# Take Back Monday

Reclaim your workweek
and live a life you love.

By Becky Burton and Robin Konie

Hear more inspiring stories and join the revolution at
**www.takebackmonday.com**

# CONTENTS

It's time for change.

INTRODUCTION

If you're holding this book in your hands, it's likely you're yearning for something more in your day-to-day work. Perhaps you're ready for relocation, inspired to pursue a long-time passion, curious about a new field, or simply convinced there must be more than surviving 9 to 5. Maybe you have an inkling that if something changed, you would no longer cringe when Sunday night comes around, followed by the world's least favorite day of the week.

For far too long we have lived with the shared acceptance that Monday is something to slog through, complain about, scorn, and vilify. Of course, it isn't only the first day of the week we dread, but what it represents: the first in a long string of days before the weekend—before we get to do what we really want.

It's time to stop wishing the week away, waiting for Friday's return.

What if every day could feel as fulfilling as the weekend? What if the line between work and your days off could be so blurred that Tuesday afternoon becomes as lovely as Sunday morning?

The good news? It's possible.

The better news? People are living this way every day.

The best news? You can, too.


This book is filled with the stories of 20 individuals who have taken the leap, made a change, and custom built a life they love. You likely won't recognize their names and, in our opinion, that's the best part of this book. These are people without fortune, pedigree, fame, or celebrity.

These are people just like you.

These are your neighbors, your friends, and your acquaintances. Maybe you know someone who also has a story worth sharing, someone who has taken risks and followed their heart despite all odds. Perhaps you've wondered, "How did they do it?" and then followed that with a deflated, "I don't know if I ever could." We hope these pages will illuminate that question and shatter its subsequent doubts by showing you what pursuing a dream actually *looks like*.

We all hear that failure is inevitable, but how do you get up again? Everyone says patience is a must, but how long do you really have to wait? We know hard work, courage, and grit are all required, but how do you muster the strength day after day? How do you stay true to yourself when others say your idea is impossible or tell you that you don't have what it takes?

The stories here answer these questions in a very real way. In fact, those we interviewed agreed to participate only if they could 'tell it like it really is.' You'll read about feelings of inadequacy, rejection, uncertainty, confusion, and fear. You'll also read about failure—lots of it. There isn't a story in this book that is smooth sailing all the way.

That said, you won't find any stories of regret either. Despite the anxiety, disappointments, and setbacks along the way, every last person would do it again.

Why? Because of the fulfillment, satisfaction, and joy that fills their day-to-day work. Because they savor the freedom that comes from calling the shots. They relish using their one-of-a-kind talents to create something unique for the world. They find confidence in knowing they've followed their intuition and are living with purpose every day of the week.

Their enthusiasm for what they do is so palpable you can gather it up like confetti and join in the celebration.

As we pull back the curtain and reveal the details that are often untold, you'll see this is not a step-by-step guide for creating a life you love. Pursuing your dreams doesn't follow a marked path. Instead of an exact blueprint, you'll find applicable lessons relevant for any plan—real-life examples of how to follow your intuition, face fear, persevere, look within, and give everything to make your vision a reality.

No matter where you are in your own journey, we hope these stories will inspire and ignite, soothe and strengthen, enlighten and embolden. We want this book to serve as a personal cheerleading squad for your own pursuits. Making the leap to follow your dreams rarely happens in isolation. You need support, guidance, and someone telling you, "Yes, you can!"

As you turn the pages of this book, we hope you'll feel you've been invited to a wonderful party where the guests are fascinating truth tellers who gently put their hand on your shoulder and say, "I've been there. I understand. It seems unthinkable now, but I'm here to tell you it's possible."

If you've ever wanted to pursue your hobby as full-time work, this book is for you. If you've ever had the feeling you're in the wrong job, pull up a chair. If you're just entering the work force and confused about which path to take, you're not alone. If you're close to retirement but ready for a change today, you're in the right place.

You can live the life you have imagined. You can conquer fears that seem indomitable. You can find engaging work that speaks to your unique passions. You can create a life that makes you eager to jump out of bed every day of the week—especially on Monday.

"Get out of the dungeon."

KATE TRACI

"As a little girl I wanted to be a princess or a witch," says Kate Traci with a mischievous smile. "I clearly remember the day I realized that my dad was not a king—it sort of deflated the whole princess idea. But that was okay. I knew being a witch would be more fun anyway."

Our adult lives rarely live up to the magical expectations of our childhoods. When we're eight, we talk about being an astronaut or a ballerina. In high school, maybe a doctor. By the time we finish college, most of us are simply looking for any job that will pay the bills.

Even though she still has hopes of becoming a witch, Kate says her life took this familiar path after college. For 11 years, she worked as a 911 dispatcher for Sacramento County. Two years into it, she knew it wasn't the job for her. She had dreams of going to graduate school or working for the FBI. But like so many people who feel stuck in their situation, she kept at it.

"After getting denied to a few graduate programs, the rejection began to take its toll. I just started to accept the fact that I was going to stay in this job forever."

Kate dubbed her working space "the dungeon." As she reflects on those days, she says, "I had some amazing moments in my career, but I lost my twenties and was beginning to lose my thirties to the dungeon." Between working graveyard shifts in a windowless room, dealing with people on their worst days, and feeling overworked and never appreciated, Kate felt her job "chipping away at her soul."

"I was not the person I used to be before the job, and it took a long time for that person to come back once I left. I knew that in order to have a life I really wanted—freedom, travel, writing—I would have to leave. It felt like I was dying a slow death in there."

For nine years Kate knew she should quit, but she needed a push to make it happen.

The push came, but in an unexpected manner.

"My mother passed away in December of 2008 after a six-month battle with cancer. It was blessedly quick for her, yet terribly too fast for us. Not enough time, never enough time.

"It was one of the hardest times of my life—balancing a full-time job with a sick mother who lived eight hours away—but my family pulled together and my mom's friends were always there helping. I never believed she really would pass away.

"I felt surrounded by love—for her, for me. Because I had to dig deeper than I ever had, I entered a new level of awareness about the things that are important. I realized how gracious and kind the universe can be and how much love we are surrounded by if we only look for it."

Though the heartache still lingers, her mother's passing served as an impetus for the change Kate needed.

"My mom was only 60 years old when she passed. 60! I realized there is never enough time to love life, to love others, to love what we do and who we are. We have to grab it when we can—and I did."

Wanting to realize the many dreams waiting for her, Kate knew what she needed to do. "After my mom passed, I made up my mind and six months later I quit the job I had worked at for more than a decade. I decided to leap. I left and have never looked back."

In 2010, Kate found herself voluntarily unemployed.

Leaving didn't mean instant gratification. She is open about the loneliness she felt during that time. She faced a lot of difficult questions. "Who am I now that I am no longer this job? How do I define myself? How do I shape my future? What do I even want to be?

"That was the big question."

Complicating the inner struggle of redefining herself was the reality of her situation. "How am I going to support myself? When I need to get a job again, what will it be? Will I fall into the same situation again? There were lots of questions going through my head," she recalls.

Kate had a plan, but it just didn't fit into the traditional mold so often expected of society. Instead of applying for new positions or jumping into her own business, Kate decided to dedicate a year to rediscovering a life she could love.

"A year of foolishness (according to some) and bravery (according to others) and adventure (according to me) was ahead. At the end of it I hoped to find something I had lost a long time ago. Me."

Kate received an inheritance after her mother's death. At first, she felt uncertain about how best to use the gift. "There was so much attached to the money. It was a struggle to know if I was using it for the right things. But I also knew there was a lot of love behind it. I knew my mom wouldn't want me to use it any other way."

After feeling poisoned by the fear that kept her stuck in a dead-end situation, Kate was determined to look fear straight in the eyes.

"I used to be such a confident girl in my twenties and something happened. Life knocked me down one too many times, I guess. I started to learn about failure and hard work and shattered dreams. Those are hard lessons. Fear definitely took hold and still does!

"After quitting my job I threw myself into doing bucket-list items, most of which were really scary."

She got certified in scuba diving, took flying lessons, started a novel, ran to raise money for cancer research, backpacked through Canada, visited the Galapagos Islands, and traveled to Italy with her dad and sister.

Kate's new job was living life as fully as possible.

A year and a half later, a renewed Kate felt ready to take on the world. "It has taken me a couple years to figure out what I was really meant to do, and how to make a living doing it," she says. She is now self-employed as a ghostwriter. She is passionate about helping shape the stories and messages of others. She also loves being able to forge her own experiences.

"Being mobile and having the autonomy to make my own decisions can be the scariest thing at times, but it is also the most freedom I have ever felt. It's pretty amazing to see something I built actually be sustainable for my life and the life I want in the future."

When asked if she'd do anything differently, she is quick to respond. "Yes, of course. A busy, productive, and fulfilling life holds many lessons along with regret. It just comes with the territory, I think.

"I would have not quit gymnastics or piano as a kid. I would have visited my mom for her last Christmas on Earth instead of being at work. I would have moved to St. Thomas when I had the opportunity. We must accept and move on."

Moving on is what Kate does best. While her family members often throw up their hands while exclaiming, "What will Kate do next?" they continue to stand behind her. Kate also feels the guiding presence of her mom. "She led me to where I am now, and I still have dreams about her. I know she is coming to check on me."

When asked what lessons life has offered, she summarizes by saying, "First, effort. Effort is the answer. Just do the work and it will be rewarded.

"Second, surround yourself with the best people. Cut everyone else loose. They aren't worth your time.

"Third, be kind. Everyone is trying hard. Just be nice."

Kate's story is the perfect answer to the age-old question, "What do you want to be when you grow up?" Instead of naming titles or rattling off job descriptions, Kate answers with a simple, "Me." While her year of adventure is inspiring, it never would have happened without the courage to leave her personal prison in the first place. Freedom only comes when we are willing to escape the things that hold the tightest grip.

Is it easy? Rarely.

Is it essential? Absolutely.

"We should obsess less about all the things we have to do, and focus more on the kind of person we want to be."

TREENA HUANG

"In today's world, with its limitless options, making confident choices can be stressful and challenging," says Treena Huang. "We're socially educated to value certain things and pursue certain goals, but we're never really taught how to evaluate what is right for us. Making difficult decisions is much easier when we know what we value and who we aspire to be."

In her daily work, Treena carefully guides others by urging them to dig deep and answer important questions: "What am I most proud of in my life?" "What kind of person do I want to be?" "How do I want to be defined?"

She does so because she herself grappled with similar questions for almost a decade.

Poised and affable, Treena is the type of person everyone loves to be around. Her exuberance for life is contagious and her openness is gently disarming. Her drive for excellence is palpable, as is her sense of diplomacy—a skill honed over 15 years as a career official at the United Nations.

If there ever was a picture-perfect job description, Treena had it. Her career path was ideal for an ambitious young professional with a desire to do good in the world—fulfilling mandates, immense opportunities for growth, travel to fascinating locales, and esteemed colleagues.

She earned coveted opportunities to work in the front offices of senior officials and serve as Head of Office to President Bill Clinton in his role as UN Special Envoy to Haiti.

She remembers her time at the UN fondly. "I couldn't say a bad thing about it. It was an incredible career and a remarkable privilege. I was meeting amazing people and doing important work." However, it is in these types of situations—when things are very good—that it is most difficult to acknowledge they may not be right.

"I was being recognized for my efforts, but I didn't feel energized by what I was doing. I was frustrated and confused by the lack of fulfillment I felt." Treena contemplated resigning, but the pull of golden handcuffs paralyzed her.

"Then I really thought about why quitting was so difficult for me. I realized I was afraid of losing the financial security and prestige. I was afraid of what others would think, afraid I wouldn't find a better job, afraid to fail. Once I recognized I was letting insecurity grip me, everything became clear. I had no idea what I would do next, but I knew that I didn't want to be someone who was motivated by fear. I had more life in me than that."

Instead, Treena chose to define herself with courage. She left a stable and esteemed career in search of a more fulfilling life. To this day, she says it is the most terrifying thing she has ever done—to leap without a plan.

"I'm the type of person who always has a plan B, as well as C, D, and E! To quit without any idea of what was next was totally out of character for me. However, I knew it was the only way to discover new options that would be intentional and conscious choices."

Her search for the right next step began by turning one of life's greatest fears—fear of the unknown—on its head. Looking back, she is able to capture her process in a few deliberate steps.

First, she based her confidence on a reliable track record.

"I embraced uncertainty by acknowledging that I was a perfectly capable person with a history of learning and adapting successfully. I came to see that within uncharted territory there are so many amazing things to discover. When I perceived it this way, it wasn't scary anymore. It was actually exciting.

"In short, I made a conscious decision to distinguish between my inside insecurities and the reality outside of myself."

Second, Treena reconnected with joy. In the months just after resigning, she spent time visiting old friends, reading, writing, practicing yoga, and playing ukulele on the beach. She also spent a month in silent meditation at a remote Thai monastery. Her time there inspired deep self-reflection that provided distance from the noise of daily life.

"Indulge in simple pleasures that spark your happiness," she advises. "When you're able to take time out to feel fulfillment in everyday things, you reawaken the dormant parts of yourself. You create space and light for new things to be discovered."

It was in this spirit of discovery that Treena pursued a lifelong curiosity about the psychology of human behavior to study neuro-linguistic programming. "I was fascinated to learn how human beings are wired, and how behavioral change happens. I wanted to understand how motivation works and what makes some people so much more effective than others.

This knowledge helped heighten my own self-awareness and motivated me to gain clarity on the kind of life I wanted, and the type of person I wanted to be. I was finally discovering how to get to 'happy.'"

With this new perspective, she worked to find fulfillment by making small shifts in her daily life and recognizing that change doesn't happen overnight. "Living out a vision requires you to repeatedly make the conscious choice to believe in yourself. No matter how challenging something may seem, you are your best investment. We invest in ourselves by making small shifts in our thinking every day."

After a two-year hiatus, Treena has returned to the UN to introduce the value of coaching to an environment she knows well. While carving out a new role there, she continues to grow a private coaching practice during the evenings and weekends.

"When I meet with clients and we achieve results together, it affirms my intuition that this is what I'm meant to be doing. Coaching allows me to connect directly with people and help them find their truth. It also holds me accountable for checking in with myself, and making sure that I'm doing the same things I encourage others to do.

"The goal is to get to a place where we stop conforming to the ideals of others, and we start living within our own. We are no longer looking outside for signs and advice. We are being guided by the inspiration that dwells inside of us."

Having worked with clients from all walks of life, Treena notes that the universal challenge to making a life change is fear.

"These significant changes are daunting, but the quickest way to access our own intelligence and act with courage is to consult the person who knows us best—our 'highest self.' This is the person who always lives by her values—the person you aspire to be. By constantly making choices based on what we value most and always keeping at the forefront the type of person we want to be, we slowly become the 'highest self'—one choice at a time."

"Step out of the assembly line."

SARAH BURROUGHS

Sophisticated, chic, and handmade. These words describe the beautiful anne b bags storming boutiques across the nation. They are also a spot-on description of the founder of anne b designs, Sarah Burroughs.

Sarah is a seamstress, designer, business owner, and champion of creativity. She's quick to educate people about the importance of handmade products in a society flooded with the mass-produced. Her love for anything artfully crafted compelled Sarah to take a step away from the assembly line of life. After going through the motions of the standard education-to-career system, Sarah is now stitching together a beautiful life all her own.

These days, you'll find her behind a sewing machine, training and employing refugees, or organizing service trips abroad. She has created a life by fusing her deepest passions.

But here's the thing: she has no formal education in any of it.

"When I was in school, I wanted to study fashion or interior design, but it was too expensive," says Sarah. Always drawn to the creative, she began her college career as a dance major. Despite being far along in her studies, deep down she felt that the dance program wasn't quite the right fit. She followed her instincts and made the difficult decision to switch majors, ultimately earning a degree in advertising.

Upon graduation, she found a job with a great company. She moved from the training department into a marketing position where she got paid to work in a field related to her major. For many people, this is the picture-perfect idea of success.

Sarah saw things differently. Even after making the switch to a "perfect" position, she realized it wasn't where she was supposed to be.

"I felt like I needed a salary job—you know, something to get me started in a real career. I tried to make it work, but it just wasn't a good fit. I knew I wanted to do something else, even though it took me a few years to really claim it."

Her love for sewing and teaching continued to surface as she considered what to do with her life. "I started making bags in college," she says. "I wanted to do something that would differentiate me from everyone else. Of course I liked the compliments I got from making bags, but it was always just a hobby for me."

Other than a brief introduction to sewing in middle-school home economics, Sarah is completely self-trained. "The first bag I made was terrible. It was not even functional. But I kept at it. I taught myself how to work with rivets, zippers, and leather. It was a lot of trial and error."

Looking at her designer bags now, you would never know she is self-taught. Each bag is artfully crafted from her workshop in Salt Lake City, and the popularity of anne b is growing fast.

The heart of Sarah's story goes beyond her beautiful products, though. Helping other people foster their own creativity is always at the forefront of her mind.

"During my junior year of college, a friend told me I should do a workshop to teach people how to make their own bags. I thought it was a nice idea—something I would consider doing in 10 or 20 years."

While on a service trip in Uganda in 2013, Sarah felt compelled to put that "nice idea" into action. She began offering sewing lessons to Ugandan women. "I realized how much I loved teaching these women how to sew. It opened up opportunities for their own creativity, and I loved seeing that.

"I actually started teaching years ago with some sewing tutorials on YouTube showing people how to make very simple stuff, and today I still get emails and comments on those videos from people in other countries. They show their work, use recycled material, and really make it their own. It's so fulfilling to witness."

Finding fulfillment is a mantra for Sarah. "In my old job, I wasn't appreciated as much as I could have been. I wasn't acknowledged for what I did. Whatever you do, make sure you feel fulfilled. That feeling carries over to every part of your life. You end up being nicer to people and just happier overall."

Committed to growing anne b, Sarah launched an Indiegogo campaign in July of 2014. After successfully raising $10,000, she taught her first official sewing workshop in Salt Lake. She held on to that momentum and left her corporate job for good.

"I love planning parties and bringing people together, so getting a group together to sew is the best of both worlds. I've met so many incredible and creative people through this work. My friend list is constantly growing. It opens up people's eyes to what they can do."

People come to her website at first to purchase bags and then learn about her workshop offerings. "When they realize they can learn how to make the bag instead of just buying it, they get excited. That's the real joy for me."

Fostering creativity ignites Sarah's enthusiasm. "So many things are mass produced today. People have lots of items that aren't really worth anything. All my products are handmade. I like to educate people on why that's important. Handmade is worth a lot more. Handmade means a lot more. And it's even better when customers take the opportunity to learn how to make their own things.

"To say, 'I made this' is empowering. It's worth more when you put your own creativity and work into something."

Sarah also loves that her story inspires others. "I love people's reactions when they hear that I left a stable job to start my own business. They always say, 'I wish I could do that,' and I tell them, '*You can!*'"

Even with her enthusiasm, Sarah acknowledges the challenges of running a successful business. Between dealing with government requirements for employing refugees, managing finances, and quickly outgrowing the space needed to do her work, Sarah is no stranger to the growing pains of entrepreneurship.

She speaks of the constant pressure to do her best and honor the mission of her company. She's very clear: it isn't always easy.

"Certain situations have really tested my ability to stay true to the vision. For example, I recently had to work through a challenging experience with one of my refugee employees. Her work wasn't matching that of the others, but she was asking for higher compensation. The situation became so emotionally challenging because I care deeply for my employees, but the cultural misunderstanding prohibited an honest dialogue. I questioned one of the core values of the business: to employ refugees."

"I just kept thinking, 'If it's right, it should be easy, and this is *hard.*' I believed in my mission, but a part of me just wanted to throw in the towel. I felt morally conflicted.

"I took some time to reflect and look at the problem from all angles. I realized that ultimately I had caused the issue by not being clear with my expectations. Communication really is the key to a good relationship—*any* relationship. We were able to work through the problem in a way that served everyone, and now I know to set clear standards and effective communication channels from the start."

The experience served as a reminder that doing what you love takes commitment. "Following your dream is going to be hard. The dream doesn't just happen. You have to take action," she says. Despite these challenges—and in some cases, *because* of them—Sarah's passion pushes through.

"If you just do it, God will provide. If it's in line with your purpose in life, He'll help. Show some faith. He will put the right people in your path, the right opportunities, the right timing— that is, if you're willing to work at it.

"I had the thought to start the business when I graduated from college. It started as a simple idea but eventually the voice in my head said, 'Sarah, you *need* to do this.' When I finally went for it, everything lined up. It all worked out. I know I'm doing what I'm supposed to be doing with my life. I wouldn't want to be anywhere else."

Sarah's business is built on the idea of stepping away from the ordinary and creating something worthwhile. She encourages and supports those wanting to escape the automated path and take a chance on their own handcrafted endeavors.

"Develop your talents," she says firmly. "Find a way to do whatever you're passionate about. It doesn't matter what people think. Don't be afraid. Get over yourself and do it.

"I did what made me unique, and I discovered this ability to merge the things I love: creating, teaching, and bringing people together. My work is part of my identity. Doing something I feel so passionate about has made all the difference."

"Trust your gut even if someone tells you it's impossible."

ROB GRABOW

It was July of 2004 with four months to go before the presidential election. Every publicist said the timeline was too short. Experts said it couldn't be done. From every corner, the response was the same: four months was simply not enough time.

Why not take a year then?

"We knew in our gut that this was a good idea and we had to do it at that moment. It couldn't wait until after the election." Even a decade later, Rob Grabow gets animated as he speaks about the necessity of the project he pursued so many years ago.

The vision? To publish an anthology of essays on social issues written by young people from across the United States. Rob and his friend, Dean Robbins, would work together on the book—soliciting submissions, editing the compilation, finding a publisher, and marketing the finished product. It all had to happen before November, though. Waiting for four years until the next election was not an option.

"We wanted to give voice to our peers," says Rob. "We were old enough to vote and serve in the armed forces, but our voices weren't being heard in the political arena."

In college, Rob was not a political science major. He had no experience in publishing or marketing. Like most undergrads, he also had no real income.

"During those months, I was living on $400 a month with $50,000 in student loan debt. I was sleeping on friends' couches and waking up with beer cans under my head and cigarette butts stuck to my arm," recalls Rob with a laugh. "It was totally crazy."

Rob is your quintessential good guy—part class clown, part valedictorian. Though he has a gentle irreverence, it shouldn't belie his deep determination to achieve. At the end of a leisurely jog with a friend, he sometimes takes off in a sprint just to see how close he can get to a four-minute mile. That's only *after* he's straightened up toppled garbage cans along the running route, though. He's not the type to sit idly by when something can be done to improve a situation.

"We asked everyone we could think of to get funding for the book. We asked our family and friends for loans, but it just wasn't possible for most of them. We approached an entrepreneurial program and were turned down. We even met with an angel-investment group but we refused their offer because the terms were so tight. They wanted 30 percent of sales and full payback of the principal. There was no way we could guarantee that at the time."

In short, there would be no financial backing for the book. They decided to proceed anyway.

"First, we needed a website for submissions. We had no experience in computer science, so we got a how-to book and taught ourselves," explains Rob.

Said this way, it sounds like a walk in the park. But then he continues. "We built the entire site and then accidentally deleted the whole thing. So, we built it again and—you'll never believe it—we deleted it a second time. Seriously, I almost lost it." There is still a hint of aggravation as he tells the story. "We worked on that thing for 36 hours straight. It took us three tries, but we finally got it going."

After the funding search and website build-out, it was already August—three months until the election.

The next step was to gather essays from 18- to 24-year-olds from across the country. Before soliciting submissions, Rob and Dean used their networks to get stories placed in local newspapers. Once the project was written up in *The Spokesman-Review* and *The Seattle Times,* they had credibility to approach others.

"Most of the school newspapers we contacted agreed to write an article. The story was published by almost 70 of them! Submissions started pouring in. We received almost 1,000 in the first few days. We were so excited. It all happened so fast."

The sheer quantity of submissions meant they had a lot of reading to do. "At this point, we were working 90 hours a week. It never felt like work, though. We were having a blast. The only break we took was to play beer pong on the weekend," he laughs.

Then they had a major breakthrough. Dean's dad saw their commitment and loaned them $15,000 to make the book a reality. They used some of the money to hire a PR firm, but the book still wasn't ready. "We had nibbles of interest from MSNBC and Fox, but both networks wanted to see the finished product."

As the election neared, they raced against the clock. "Friends were invaluable at this time," Rob recalls. "One was a brilliant copyeditor and stayed up all night editing the book. Another friend helped us self-publish by learning a layout program from scratch, just from the goodness of her heart. I think when people see that something matters to you, they want to be part of it. When your intent is genuine, people rally around you.

"My mom's encouragement was also huge," he adds. "Even though I had massive student loans, she stood behind me when I turned down a job offer that came through during this time. She told me to listen to my gut. She reminded me that life is short."

By October 25, all of the work and encouragement paid off. In spite of warnings to the contrary, they had met their production goal. The book was ready. They had compiled and edited the country's first non-partisan political anthology by young people.

The final step was to get exposure—in less than a week.

During this critical time, Rob's mom called while she was watching election coverage. "Seventy-year-olds are talking about young voters on CNN right now, acting as authorities on who you are and what you want," she told him.

Rob knew their PR firm had the contact information of the top producer at CNN. He admits to being a little tipsy when sending an email to challenge the network's coverage and demanding to know, "Why are older people allowed to speak on our behalf?"

Two days later, the CNN producer called and asked if they could be at the studio the next morning to talk about their story. Rob remembers running to find Dean. "We completely freaked out. It was right before the election. Our books were printed and we were ready to go. We were thrilled."

After the appearance on CNN, MSNBC interviewed them. A month later, after the elections were over, they appeared for an hour-long session on CSPAN's Book TV.

"It might have been impossible for all the publishers and publicists, but it wasn't impossible for two motivated college kids." Rob's voice carries in it a gentle pride. Then he admits, "You know, the book never made money. But that was never our goal. Our vision had always been to give voice to young Americans. We definitely did that."

While this story is a snapshot in time, it represents Rob's broader approach to life.

Today, he owns a multi-million-dollar sportswear company he founded as a sophomore in college. He also holds a master's degree in international affairs from Columbia University, where he graduated in 2011. His drive to understand global economics and foreign policy was as strong as his ambitions to start an affordable sportswear company and publish the anthology years earlier. This same inner drive is now propelling Rob to master a new skill—acting. He is preparing to move to New York for an intensive acting program after several months of part-time theater study in Seattle.

Rob's story provides a critical lesson—it is not necessary to only find one passion and pursue it indefinitely. His experiences show that life can be a journey of pursuing many different things.

Three lessons Rob learned during the anthology project continue to guide him today.

"First, follow your passion. If you have an idea and it matters to you, just do it.

"Second, there is no substitute for working your tail off. Put in the hours. Work as long as it takes. Don't get distracted. Do what you want to do.

"Third, it is fantastic to have a support group. It makes the whole process more fun. That is where a lot of the meaning will come from."

As an outside observer, one sees a fourth lesson in Rob's success. He takes any excuse and politely tosses it out the window. He didn't let a tight timeline stand in his way, nor student loans, nor lack of early funding. He wasn't deterred by limited technical expertise or having to start over on the website more than once. He reached out to those who could help, even though it may have been uncomfortable at the time. He held on to his vision and didn't let anyone's notion of impossibility stand in the way.

"Time marches on whether you make
a change or not. The question is,
what are you going to do with that time?"

SARAH BURTON

Drawings of lopsided houses and stick figures with seven fingers decorate the walls of Ms. Burton's classroom. It's a stark contrast to the sleek logos and glossy advertisements that lined the halls of her old job. Transitioning from a graphic designer to an elementary school teacher is not a classic career trajectory, but for Sarah Burton, it was the right one.

"I'd been at my job for quite a while and was beginning to feel that there wasn't any progression," she says. "I didn't *mind* going, but I didn't really *like* it either. There wasn't daily satisfaction. Above all, I felt I wasn't contributing to the world in a way that was bigger than myself."

At 36 years old, Sarah faced the question many kindergarteners are asked to consider: "What do you want to do with your life?"

"When you're nearing 40, this is a very tough question. I had so many financial obligations and I had earned my first degree decades earlier."

During this time, Sarah volunteered a few hours each week teaching English to adults. "I felt so much fulfillment throughout those evenings spent with my students. There was a sense of mutual satisfaction when my students learned new ways to express themselves. I wanted my everyday job to feel as fulfilling as the short time each week I spent tutoring.

"As it was, my workdays were just about getting from 8 to 5. That is fine for some people, but I needed to be doing more for the world."

Sarah describes the moment she knew teaching was the answer: "It just came to me one morning after I'd been thinking for months about the different options I could pursue.

"It wasn't a flash of inspiration, per se, but so many parts of my personal history aligned at that moment. There was the volunteering, of course, and I also reflected on all of my teachers growing up and the immense impact they had on my life. I thought back to my early days of university when teaching had been an interest, but so many in my family were teachers and I had wanted to take a different path.

"More than anything, I just had an undeniable feeling that it was right."

No matter how certain the conviction, it doesn't diminish the fear that accompanies a major life change.

"There were so many scary moments once I knew I wanted to get a degree in education," Sarah admits. "I was leaving a career I was good at and a job that was comfortable. I wasn't even sure if I would like teaching! What if I was horrible at it or hated it? Then I would have taken on this big risk—not to mention the student loans—and be in the same place as before. I was also afraid of not being successful in my studies because I hadn't been a student for so long."

Sarah coped with the fear by honoring her intuition. "I knew it was going to be hard, but I also knew a change was necessary."

Advice from a family friend helped her stay the course. "Time is going to keep marching forward whether you make the change now or not, so you may as well do it now. It's the only way you'll be where you want to be in a year rather than wondering what might have been."

Sarah knew herself well enough to recognize she needed to go all in if she were to be successful. She applied to a prestigious master's program—a three-semester intensive requiring full-time study. "My intuition told me the program was the right fit for me. I explored online options, but I knew I wanted to be on a campus. However, the program required me to quit my job and study full-time. There were no night classes. I had very little savings and the thought of giving up a steady income was frightening."

To this day, however, she knows it was the best option. "If I had chosen something else, I might not have gone all the way through. I needed the momentum of studying all the time, every day."

In figuring out the pieces of her financial puzzle, Sarah learned an important lesson. "I had to ask my parents for financial support. I hadn't asked them for money in over 20 years! However, they taught me the importance of asking for help when you need it. When you ask, you find people want to help. You're giving them a chance to be part of your journey."

Still, Sarah knew most of the journey would be hers to take alone. As an avid runner, she compares her time in school to finishing a marathon.

"Lots of people believe in you, but you really have to get behind yourself and be your own support system. If you aren't the one moving your legs, you won't finish.

"The only way to make it is to keep the end goal in mind. The first step is the hardest, but then you keep checking things off the list and before you know it, you're thousands of steps in and you're almost at your destination.

"There are times when you simply have to work really, really, really hard. But when you finish, you don't dwell on the difficulty of the race. You dwell on the fact that you made it to the end.

"That is my biggest piece of advice. Keep pushing through because the end will come. It may seem miles away in the beginning, but it will come. Pushing through is the only way to reach the end goal."

Now, after almost a year of teaching, every day is like crossing the finish line for Sarah. She begins each morning by sitting with a group of third graders anxious to participate with hands held high, ready to share their ideas, reflections, and aspirations. Their curiosity about the world invokes her own sense of wonder. Every day she teaches new concepts, like the principles of inertia or the definition of determination—ideas that have propelled her own progress.

No longer soldiering through the day to make it to 5 p.m., Sarah finds that each moment feels new and different. The sense of fulfillment remains the same, though. "I love going into my classroom every morning and being there throughout the day. Even when I need to stay late, I never mind being there. Each day is filled with learning something new. Every day I am changing lives for the better."

Most importantly, she has found her own answer to the age-old question, "What do you want to do with your life?"

"It took some time to get here," she says, "but I'm glad my own journey unfolded this way. You can always look back and wish you started earlier. For me, I needed to explore other options first and they have all enriched my teaching. I wouldn't go back and do anything differently because I love the way it all turned out."

Sarah's story offers lessons for anyone, from a degree-seeking freshman to a mid-career professional. You must be brave enough to alter course when the road is no longer leading you where you want to go. The new route may seem scary with unfamiliar twists and turns, but if your intuition guides you down a different path, you can be sure the vista at the end will be worth the journey.

"What would you
do if you couldn't fail?"

MEREDITH HUTCHISON

A young girl's eyes shine above a surgical mask. A teenager dons a hardhat and reviews blueprints. Another holds a professional camera like she was born to capture the world.

One cannot view the images of these young Congolese women without feeling a sense of triumph. Their bright faces light up the frame with a sense of all that is possible. There is fire behind their eyes, along with pride, compassion, and yearning.

They are part of a program titled *Vision Not Victim.*

In the program, girls are taken through a series of workshops to explore their aspirations for the future, meet mentors who shine a light on new possibilities, and build critical life and leadership skills needed to pursue their goals. Very few of these girls have ever been asked before, "What do you want to do with your life?" Participants are prompted to imagine what they want for their future, then create a plan to make it a reality.

The experience culminates in a photo shoot with the girls posing as their future selves, their own role models. Using props, costumes, and sets, each portrait captures an inspiring scene of the young woman trying on her future.

The girls transform into fashion photographers, journalists, doctors, and architects. One 16-year-old commands the room as the future Minister of Defense and Human Rights of the Congo, a position that doesn't exist in reality—yet. Talk about vision.

Talk about vision, indeed. Less than three years ago, this program was only the spark of an idea. Since that time, thousands of people throughout the United States and Europe have seen these photographs. Exhibits have been held in San Francisco,

New York, DC, London, and Brussels, usually in tandem with a high-profile event addressing gender inequity.

*Vision Not Victim* is the brainchild of Meredith Hutchison, a photographer with a commitment to women's rights. In her words, the goal of the project is to "produce a new generation of images in advocacy, redefine how women are portrayed in media, and give individuals—women and girls especially—greater power over how they are represented to their community, to their peers, and to the world."

If you sit down for a conversation with Meredith, you will likely do much of the talking. Her earnest eyes and focused questions create an atmosphere of comfort and calm. She nurtures a space where one can discuss both dreams and shortcomings—all without judgment. When she does speak, her message is one of encouragement and hope.

A talent for active listening has always been one of her strengths. In part, it comes from her own journey toward fulfillment.

After graduating with a master's degree from Columbia in 2011, Meredith struggled to find full-time work. She speaks openly about the depression she faced during this period, and the confusion about what she truly wanted to achieve in life.

It was during those interim months—amidst the uncertainty—that she conceived the *Vision Not Victim* concept.

"At the time, I was doing anything I could to keep my mind busy," she recalls. "I studied everything that interested me. I watched lectures about a range of topics—anything from literary analysis to physics. In the end, this worked to my advantage. I began to understand that creativity and new ideas can come from the fringe where very distinct and often isolated ideas are allowed to interact."

A new idea was born out of this time of discovery. She planned to travel to regions of crisis where women and girls are the most marginalized, and support them in creating images that communicated their ideas, priorities, and visions—images that demonstrated their power and potential—images that broke down stereotypes and social norms—images that gave a glimpse of what gender equality could look like in the future.

From the earliest days, Meredith's success came from following her intuition. She knew her idea was worthwhile. She'd done a lot of research and felt confident it was a unique approach to women's issues and communications, as well as a necessary perspective to share with the world.

She distinctly recalls the moment when she decided to pursue her vision. She laughs as she tells the story. "It's embarrassingly cheesy. It was literally a Hallmark moment!

"One day, I was at a bookstore buying a greeting card for a friend and I came across one that read: 'What would you do if you couldn't fail?'

"I thought, why would I do anything other than explore this idea? I knew where I wanted to go in my artistic and professional life and I knew it wasn't the traditional path. I decided that even if I failed, it wouldn't negate the point of having tried. I knew I needed to pursue the idea regardless of what the outcome might be.

"My support network was key during this time. I am fortunate to have family and friends who encouraged me. I remember standing on the subway platform in New York and telling two friends about my idea. I was finally getting job offers at this point in time, but considering turning them down to launch a crowdsourced fundraiser for *Vision Not Victim*. They told me to go for it."

Meredith did decline the job offers and took up a host of odd jobs to support herself instead—anything that would allow her enough to get by, but give her the time she needed to develop the concept. She launched an Indiegogo campaign in July of 2012. The crowdsourcing effort was successful.

Meredith knew, however, that to implement her idea ethically and safely in Congo—a region in conflict—she would need an experienced organizational partner.

She spent weeks submitting proposals and writing emails.

"Everyone tells you that you'll have to work hard to pursue your passion, but working hard isn't the most difficult part—at least it wasn't for me," she says. "It is the emotional roller coaster. When you start out alone, the work can be isolating and exhausting. The rejection can be especially trying.

"Questions started creeping in, even once I knew what I wanted to do. How can I pay rent? Why did this organization reject me? Am I doing the right thing?"

It was after a long search that Meredith received a reply from the International Rescue Committee—one of the world's largest and most reputable nonprofits, with an extensive network. They had been working in Congo for decades and were interested in this new approach to communication and representing women and girls.

"I met with so many organizations and people," Meredith remembers, "but when I met with my counterparts at IRC, they got it right away and had feedback, ideas, and insights to add."

"Trust your gut," she advises. "Know when you have a great idea and pursue it. Use your instincts to guide you on who your greatest allies will be."

By January of 2013, Meredith was in Congo, in partnership with the IRC, working with a group of girls on the first *Vision Not Victim* program and series of photographs.

After several successful exhibits of those first photographs in Europe and the United States, Meredith and the team embarked on the second series. In late 2014, she traveled to Jordan and worked with Syrian refugees and Jordanian girls, which culminated in a new set of vision images. Planning is now underway to strategically share these photographs.

Currently, Meredith is working with the IRC in New York on plans to implement *Vision Not Victim* in several more locations, including with resettled refugees in the United States.

Perhaps one of the most important lessons from this story is that Meredith wholeheartedly embodies the concept she works on with the girls. She envisioned exactly what she wanted to do and then made it happen. Within three years, she went from working odd jobs in New York to running a robust program and sharing her work with thousands.

When asked if she would do anything differently, Meredith's response is a humble "no."

"That's not to say I didn't make a lot of mistakes," she clarifies, "but I learned so much from them that I wouldn't have done anything differently."

Then she reconsiders and adds, "I wish I had not underestimated the opportunities we would have after the first project was complete. We only worked on photographs during our time in the Congo and I wished I would have thought more deeply about the larger vision. If I had, I would have taken more video footage and developed a stronger system of accountability to the girls. We sent them over 2,000 messages from exhibit attendees, but I would have developed a way to stay in touch over the long term. We're working on that now in future iterations.

"Before you start, talk to other people about your idea and expand the possibilities around your core. That is one of the most important lessons I learned."

Beyond this project-specific lesson, Meredith shares invaluable insights for anyone working to bring an idea to life.

"The way you treat the people around you will get you far. Know your strengths and use them to put people first. As a photographer, my technical skills aren't expert, but opportunities have come because I like people and I make them comfortable. I love to listen to them. It's because of this that they let me in and that relationship allows me to take the images I do. Put people first, not product.

"Go into any assignment reminding yourself why it is important and what needs to be achieved. There are times when I could take a great photo, but it wouldn't have helped the person in the image, nor would it have had any sort of advocacy effect afterward. It could endanger the trust I seek to build. I'm not a photojournalist for a reason. I want to build relationships.

"Learn how to ask questions. I meet so few people who know how to ask really great questions. If you want to be part of the conversation and you don't have the expertise, inquire in a way that relays your curiosity.

"Let people put their handprint on what you're doing. You have to own it, but allow others to be part of what you create.

"Trust your instincts. Always."

In speaking about the aspects she enjoys most about her current path, Meredith says, "I love that I get to work in a creative way with amazing girls on issues of women's rights. It is wonderful to work through an imaginative process with these young women who teach me so much. I love having the opportunity to engage with different kinds of people. I love thinking about the many different ways to address issues using new processes that we *haven't* tried. There is so much to do in so many ways that haven't been attempted yet."

It is clear that Meredith's life will be filled with pursuing new ideas. By looking at the fringes and listening deeply, she has honed a unique set of skills to help her create quickly and recognize a good idea. Above all, Meredith has learned to stay true to herself and pursue her ideas, whether fear of failure enters the picture or not.

"Get out of your comfort zone."

ALLEGRA STEIN

As human beings, we have an inherent desire to reach out and help others in need. This call to serve has driven countless individuals to volunteer and join service organizations in hopes of solving some of the most pressing needs around the globe. It's an experience that inherently requires a selfless heart. Or, so you would think.

"To this day I consider my decision to join the Peace Corps the most selfish decision I have ever made," says Allegra Stein.

"People don't get it, but I stand behind that statement. For me there was a deeply personal motivation for joining. I knew I had to do it for myself. I needed to discover who I was and what I was capable of."

Born and raised in Los Angeles, Allegra got her first taste of travel during a semester abroad in college. Now, her life reads like an adventure novel that has taken her across the globe— from Thailand to Nepal, Bulgaria to New York.

But her story isn't about the thrill of travel or living an exotic life.

Rather, Allegra's story is about being willing to step away from the familiar to discover her own life's mission. By uprooting herself, she developed an inner confidence. Moving away from her home in California helped her discover a home within herself.

"I knew that in order to grow and truly discover myself and what I was capable of, I had to leave behind what was comfortable and secure, and go off into the unknown."

The decision to join the Peace Corps set Allegra on a defining path that would ultimately help her lift others in significant ways. When she left her sunny home in southern California to serve 27 months in Bulgaria, she was keenly aware of what she was about to leave behind.

"Leaving my friends, family, and a relationship was hard," she recalls. "It was like a two-sided coin. Leaving, on the one side, was very difficult. However, the idea of going, on the other side, was incredibly exciting, invigorating, and inspiring. I guess I chose to focus more on the going part."

The inspiration to go fueled her spirit through the challenges she faced. Being thrown into a new culture and language, and leaving familiar conveniences was anything but easy. "It probably took a year to really feel connected to the community," she says. "Until I was more fluent in the language, it was hard to engage with my Bulgarian colleagues on a professional level. It was hard to express who I was. There was a long period of disconnectedness."

So why go? Why leave the familiar and the people you know and love?

"I was acutely aware that if I didn't take this journey, fueled by my desire to grow and explore, that I would never feel complete. If I never felt complete, I'd never be able to give myself fully to other people in the way that I wanted. I had to feed my spirit before I could feed my relationships in a positive and complete way."

So, maybe not so selfish after all. Having fed her spirit, Allegra came back from the Peace Corps with a heart ready to feed others.

"After I returned home, a friend emailed me some information about the Teach for America program that really caught my interest. I studied biology in college, but had taken a course in education during my last quarter of school. Between that class and the experiences of the Peace Corps, I felt compelled to do something in the field of education.

"I applied to the program and listed two California cities as my top choices. I thought I wanted to stay near my family and friends for a little while after being far away for so long. I was accepted into the program, but they sent me to my third choice: New York."

Forced out of her comfort zone for a second time, Allegra uprooted again and moved across the country.

"That was another defining moment in my life. As with my move to Bulgaria, I discovered so much about myself through living in a new, unknown place. When nothing is familiar or secure, you're forced to find comfort within yourself—which is where it resides anyway," she says.

For some people, the confidence needed to make such bold moves seems out of reach. People balk at the courage needed to transplant their lives somewhere new and unfamiliar.

Allegra is quick to remind that "confidence is a result of action, not a requirement for it." She says, "Whether you want more confidence, clarity, motivation, resiliency, or readiness, the solution is always the same: take action first! I was scared. What mattered is that I took the leap despite that."

Today, you will find Allegra still in New York with her family, where she now educates and inspires as a life coach.

"I found a certification program for coaching that resonated with me not long after my daughter was born. Everything since then has just fallen into place. All of my past experiences have aligned. Being a coach is the perfect culmination of all the defining moments of my life. I've been a life coach for three years now and love it."

One of Allegra's specialties is supporting others through relocation. Over the past several months, she's broadened her reach to encourage people wanting to create other big changes in their lives. "Sometimes that involves travel. Other times it's a project, business, or movement. Each experience requires stepping out of the comfort zone. I love to support people in that process and help them create a life they love."

When asked if she would do anything differently, she says, "No. Everything I've ever done and chosen has led me to this moment, so it's all good.

"I love that I have been able to discover a purpose that lights me up and creates prosperity by following that path. I love my clients and am excited to believe in them even when they themselves have a hard time seeing it."

Allegra's clarity and confidence are rooted in a life of action and have been nourished with a willingness to step out of the comfortable. When you make the climb to higher ground, you not only get a better view of the person you were meant to be, but you are more able to help others take the same journey.

"Take time to step back and consider what you really want in life."

DALE MAJORS

Six weeks touring on a bicycle provides a lot of time to ponder important questions. For Dale Majors, a long-distance bike tour from Canada to Mexico was the perfect opportunity to reflect on what he wanted for his future career.

Dale was working in multilevel marketing when he took a break to pedal 1900 miles down the Pacific coast. During long hours in the saddle, he contemplated the vision he had for his life. Though he didn't fully realize it until returning to his day-to-day work, his job in marketing didn't align with his aspirations for the future.

Around the same time, he was carefully considering the potential expansion of a small online business he'd started in high school. He believed if he dedicated himself fully to growing the company, it could be the path to the life he envisioned. It would be a risk, but one he was willing to take.

In choosing to quit the marketing firm, he was able to leave behind aspects of work that didn't align with his personal values. For starters, he hated recruiting people to a job where statistics said 99 percent of them would fail. "I couldn't bring people in knowing so few would make it," he recalls.

Now he is able to guide his employees toward long-term success by working to ensure they love their jobs through opportunities to grow right alongside the business.

In fact, Dale's commitment to job satisfaction extends beyond the four walls of his warehouse. He believes it is possible for anyone to find deep fulfillment in everyday work by considering the key question, "What do I want my life to look like?"

By asking himself this question early on, Dale was able to set his own definition of success and then work toward achieving it.

"My first goal was a financial one. I wanted to match my father's salary while still in college because it seemed a solid benchmark. Once I reached that figure, however, I found the money didn't make me any happier. It was an early lesson to evaluate exactly what I wanted my life to look like, not just how much money I wanted in the bank.

"You must be guided by what you deem is important. You will often get what you want, so you must really consider exactly what that means for you personally."

During his six-week bike trip, Dale learned how much he valued the ability to travel for long periods of time. He knew what he desired most was freedom to do what he loved. Holding this new goal as paramount, he wanted to structure the company in a way that allowed him to pursue his passions both within the business and outside of it.

Before that goal could be achieved, however, the company needed to get on solid footing.

When Dale launched Bikewagon with his father in 2004, they quickly bought up thousands of dollars in bike parts as inventory. However, in those early days, Dale was still attending college and didn't have much time to post the items for sale. As such, purchases far outpaced sales and they were afraid the extra product would sink the tiny venture. Things started to get tense.

Determined to see the business succeed, Dale decided to spend his early morning hours listing the extensive inventory until everything was posted. He committed to waking at 2 a.m. each morning and working until he left for school. Day after day he began his workday when many of his fellow students were just falling asleep. For months he followed this routine with total dedication.

"I was on fire! I knew what had to be done and no one else was going to do it. I pulled out all the stops. It was the most motivated I have ever felt in my life. It was driven by a desire to prove that we'd succeed no matter what got in the way.

"I loved this period and the roller-coaster sensation of it. It was exciting and I felt incredibly energized."

It was a decisive moment in the company's history. Without that drive, Bikewagon would not have achieved the pace of growth it has experienced. This early commitment set the trajectory for what is now a multi-million dollar business with nearly 30 employees.

For anyone in a similar situation, Dale offers this advice: "You must be willing to give total commitment. You have to think about what that really looks like to you, and usually it doesn't look like showing up from 8 to 5. It may be that you wake up at 4 a.m. and don't leave until the work is done. Ask yourself, 'What does it look like to be completely committed to this goal? What will those on the outside looking in see me doing?'

"Putting in the time will hide a lot of your shortcomings. It's important to do something that draws on your natural skills, but hard work and extra time can make up for the areas where you fall short."

In speaking of his own shortcomings, Dale wraps them up in a bundle—inexperience.

Like many entrepreneurs, he didn't have special training in all of the areas he now oversees. "In looking back, I would have done many things differently," he admits. "However, everything we did was necessary to learn the lessons we needed to learn. If I had the chance to start over but had to give those lessons in exchange, I wouldn't do it."

Experience hasn't been his only teacher. Dale constantly seeks to learn from fellow entrepreneurs and past professors. "I try to find qualified people and spill my guts to them," he says with a smile. "What I mean is that I'm transparent and open about the challenges I'm facing. I become really vulnerable and honest. The expert you're speaking to will only be able to give you worthwhile advice if he has a lot of context."

Most people Dale approaches are willing to help. When reaching out, he acknowledges the importance of their time and offers to do whatever is necessary to make the meeting convenient. "A lot of experts are willing to offer guidance. If you're taking action and making an effort, they know their advice will fall on fertile ground."

Ongoing improvement and change are vital for Dale. When it's not coming from direct experience or others in the field, he's listening to audio books to continue learning.

"One thing that has helped me to grow my business and make decisions is a tip I learned in Brian Tracy's book, *Goals! How to Get Everything You Want—Faster Than You Ever Thought Possible.* In the book, Tracy describes 'zero based thinking.' If you could go back to an early decision and make it again—knowing what you know now—would you make the decision differently? For example, knowing what you know now about your job, would you take the offer to work in the same position again? If the answer is yes, it is likely that you're on the right track. If not, then the best move may be to make a change."

Taking the time to ask himself these types of questions has allowed Dale to lead the life he envisioned so many years ago. While still actively growing the company, he leaves regularly to balance work and personal time. He and his wife recently spent a summer biking 1300 miles across Europe with their three children.

"So many people live with the notion that they just have to trudge through work until retirement. Or, they are simply 'go, go, go' and 'win, win, win' but they don't know why.

"Take time to step back and consider what you really want out of life. Once you've taken the time to ponder that question, believe that your vision is possible and commit to making it a reality."

"Do what's right for you,
not what's right for someone else."

MARILEE KILLPACK

"My mother was perfection," says Marilee Killpack. "She never worked a day in her life. In fact, there was only one day I remember coming home from school when she wasn't there. I cried that day."

Marilee is a mother, wife, and woman of deep faith. She is also an entrepreneur.

"I have always wanted to start a business," she says. "I remember selling ramen noodles at the dance studio where I took classes. I got them at Costco for 75 cents and sold them for a dollar."

Despite her early craving for business, she never planned to be where she is today. Marilee now runs a successful company— Let's Playground—selling beautiful multi-purpose floor mats. "Our leather mats can be used for indoor or outdoor play. Take them for a picnic, use them at the beach, and keep messes contained under a high chair. The mats serve as a place to gather, play, and experience life. We wanted to create a product that connects people."

From concept to thriving brand, Let's Playground has grown up fast. Unlike most businesses that start with an idea for a product, however, Marilee and her co-founder Jeni had no clue what they wanted to do when they first started.

"Jeni and I were friends growing up," Marilee says. "She moved far away while we were in middle school, but we reconnected in college. One day, out of the blue, Jeni said, 'Hey, want to start a business?' I said, 'Sure!'"

With only a firm plan to start *something*, the duo began brainstorming for the right idea.

"Jeni had a vinyl mat for play time with her baby. It was useful, but not the prettiest thing you've ever seen. We both felt like there was potential to make a functional, beautiful mat."

Even with an idea in mind, they still had a lot of work ahead of them. "Our biggest challenge was finding the right material and the right manufacturer. Without those things, we didn't have a product or a business.

"We went to LA to find fabric. We knew we wanted to work with leather, but finding the right surface and the right colors is tricky when you are limited to samples." They finally found their dream material in the form of bonded leather. "It's lightweight, easy to clean, compact, and gorgeous."

The right material was only half the equation. Making the mats was another huge challenge. "We live in a tiny house— fewer than 600 square feet. I have two small children and the mats are big—like seven-feet big. I actually know a lot about sewing, so I knew I could make the mats, but I didn't want the manufacturing part of the business to consume my life."

They found a local manufacturer in their hometown of Provo, Utah, and placed their first order for 90 mats.

"In the back of our minds, we knew we wanted to try a Kickstarter campaign, but we decided to first test the market. We didn't know if anyone was interested in what we were offering, so we decided to sell our first batch at a small local market. In one day we sold almost 40! People wanted our product, so we jumped on launching a fundraising campaign."

The crowdfunding process was anything but breezy. "You only get one chance with Kickstarter so we wanted to nail it," says Marilee. Their initial goal to launch the campaign in August of 2014 was delayed to September, then October, then November. "Everything just took longer than we expected, but we knew we needed to do it right. We finally launched on November 18."

Marilee's personal Instagram feed highlighted the beginning of their campaign journey: "It's live, ladies and gentlemen!!! And I have more butterflies than I have ever had in my whole life."

They reached their initial goal of $15,500 a day after the campaign started. The momentum for Let's Playground continued. Their project became a staff pick on Kickstarter and the final amount pledged exceeded $78,000.

"Kickstarter was reaffirming," Marilee reflects. But despite their early success, she still had a personal battle to conquer.

"I've really struggled with the idea of wanting to work. Almost every day I wonder, 'Am I a bad mom? How do I balance running this business with raising my kids?'"

Her own cherished memories of her childhood and mother often collide with her passion for creating a business she loves. "There were times before Kickstarter when I thought it would be easier to just quit. But I felt really right about pursuing this business. Everything kept falling into place. I believe it was divinely inspired."

Balancing motherhood with her new business hasn't been easy. "There is no perfect balance," she says. "I've been reading a lot of articles by business owners who are also mothers and they always say it isn't easy. But somehow you think your situation will be different.

"I've finally found a balance. I work a lot at night, after the kids have gone to bed. We've also hired some help with the kids for a couple hours each week to ensure they are getting out of the house and having meaningful experiences. Otherwise I try to live by the rule: don't work and be a mom at the same time. When I try to do both simultaneously I generally don't do either very well.

"Some days the work spills over, and I'm okay with that every now and then because I think it's important for my kids to see me doing something I love.

"The best advice I've heard on the matter is to remember that we own the business. The business doesn't own us."

She still struggles to find balance, and the idea of what she is "supposed" to be as a mother still fuels fears every now and then—but she is working on it.

"You have to get over those hurdles. It's a good thing. There are a lot of unknowns. You worry about breaking the mold, or leaving your comfort zone, or doing things differently than others. It will be stressful at times, but if it feels right, you have to do it."

When asked what she loves most about her life, she firmly says, "First, my family. Second, my beliefs. Those two things will always be my rock.

"I also love that recently I've been able to work alongside my husband more. We love working together. It's like a love language for us. That's always been the dream. To have this business be the method for the realization of that dream is so special."

When asked what lessons she's gained through the experience, she says, "When you start trying, great things will happen. You can't just talk about it. You have to jump in and do it. Even when you hit a roadblock, you can't stop. Keep trying and it will work out.

"I also learned that humanity is good. We were so overwhelmed by the outpouring of support and community that we felt since diving into this project. So often the business world is projected as cold and heartless, but our experience has shown there are a lot of good people out there."

Her final lesson is perhaps the most important, mostly because it speaks to her personal struggle. "When you do find what you are supposed to be doing—doing what feels right deep within your gut—you need to follow through. It will be hard, but it will also be fulfilling."

Marilee's children won't have the same image of their mother that Marilee had growing up, and that's okay. The perfect mom isn't necessarily the one who stays home, nor is it the one who creates a successful business. The perfect mom is the one who finds her own path and lives her right life. Being happy is a legacy worth giving your children. Without a doubt, Marilee's children will look back and see their own version of "perfection."

"Change tends to cloak itself as risk, but welcoming change is the only way to grow."

BRENDAN SAPIENCE

In January 2014, one goal was front and center in Brendan Sapience's mind—to move from Hong Kong to the United States by year's end.

He wasn't looking to change career paths with the geographical shift. In fact, Brendan loved his job. "I think working for a tech company is fantastic," he says. "Our market is complex and rich with an ever-changing range of technologies and players."

Instead, he knew a transfer within his company was the ideal next step.

A software engineer by training and driven by what he terms a "bottomless curiosity," Brendan feels that the field of information technology is a perfect fit for him. The current momentum for innovation within the sphere provides endless opportunities for discovery.

A new position would bring unique challenges and continuous learning. The new locale also meant he would finally live near his girlfriend in Canada.

After discussions with senior management, it became clear the transition made sense for the company, too. Given his years of experience at the firm, Brendan was well placed to help the business grow stateside. It was shaping up to be a winning scenario on all fronts.

By May, he was offered a position in Boston and everything began to fall into place. Brendan gave notice to his landlord, shared the news with friends, and started packing.

Just as he was about to sign his contract, however, unexpected news brought the plan to a grinding halt. A direct competitor was planning to buy the company he worked for.

"This wasn't good news at all," he remembers. "The people with the executive power to finish my transfer were no longer in charge. My champions—the influential people rooting for my transition abroad—were no longer listened to. We all became strangers in a new world. I was suddenly anonymous to the influential players. I became just another name and job title on the payroll."

As Brendan looked around, he noticed his colleagues handled the buyout in one of three ways. The resigned passively accepted the change and adapted over time. The frustrated blamed the new company for obstacles and bedeviled it for changing things. The resilient dedicated energy to navigating the unfamiliar maze until they found their best fit in the new system or moved on.

Brendan resolved to be part of the final group. With arrangements to leave Hong Kong already set in motion and no desire to return to his native France, he knew the quickest way to the United States would be through a new position within the company.

"Our firm had bought companies before and I had witnessed, without ever living it, the many pitfalls of being on the 'wrong side of the fence.' I knew what I needed to do. I had to carefully engineer my way through the buyout by custom building a reputation for myself as quickly as possible.

"How did I do it? By knowing exactly which priorities to focus on, then dedicating a lot of energy to those things."

He spent the first few hours after the announcement gathering as much information as possible about the new players. "I started my work right away by making sense of who did what, who had authority and where, and which players were connected to each other."

During the first month, he attended every possible event and engaged with each new contact. "With so many new faces, titles, and other things to learn, it became crucial to observe everything," Brendan recalls. "I attended all the meetings I could, no matter what they were about and no matter what time they were at." He often woke in the middle of the night to attend conference calls organized by the headquarters in Europe and the United States.

"I made sure to ask plenty of smart questions. Then I reached out to all of the relevant people and let them know who I was in a memorable way."

Eventually, Brendan was invited to a meeting at the US headquarters. Jetlagged after a 20-hour flight, he was asked to give an impromptu demonstration of his old company's software. It wasn't the easiest task given his state of exhaustion, but he did it successfully and made a solid impression in front of a key audience.

"That test didn't happen by chance," he reveals with a smile. "I planted the idea of that demonstration the day before by mentioning it to several people. I knew it would be a challenge, but I also knew it would be an excellent way to show them what I could do."

Brendan was then invited to a larger meeting in Paris with the senior management. "Again, I asked a lot of questions and answered questions. I made comments and volunteered to take on tasks—some I successfully completed, some I failed at."

Most importantly, by the end of the session, the chief sales officer knew who Brendan was. After the meeting, he received an email from one of the people who mattered most. The head of sales in the United States sent a message congratulating his performance.

His months of dedication, extra hours, attention to detail, and perseverance had paid off. He was offered a position with the US team and moved into a Manhattan apartment in early December. With New York City at his feet and his girlfriend only an hour's flight away, he couldn't be happier with how everything turned out.

Reflecting on his experience, Brendan recognizes that success can often come from embracing disruption. "Change tends to cloak itself as risk," he muses, "but welcoming change is the only way to grow. An experience that consists of only doing things you already know how to do isn't an opportunity; it is just a continuation.

"Whenever you are offered an opportunity that you are hesitant about because you don't know if you'll be good enough for it, take it. You will figure out the details later. 'Mount Insurmountable' can always be conquered by incremental effort as long as you are persistent and fueled with passion and commitment."

Though he could have easily allowed the buyout to thwart his personal aspirations, Brendan chose to recognize the sudden change as a moment to test himself within a new context. Not only was he driven by an unwavering commitment to his goals, he was also motivated by the potential to transform the unexpected into an opportunity that far exceeded his own expectations.

"Keep moving forward,
even if you're afraid."

STEPHANIE GAUDREAU

Make no mistake about it—Stephanie Gaudreau is powerful.

As the owner of the website Stupid Easy Paleo, Steph knows a thing or two about nutrition and healthy living. She's created a community of enthusiasts who are dedicated to eating nourishing whole foods, lifting heavy things above their heads, and who strive to be "healthy, happy, and harder to kill." As an Olympic-style weightlifter and avid fitness enthusiast, Steph is as strong as she is business savvy.

Not too long ago, however, she was living a very different life. Before making a powerful and authoritative impression in the Paleo world, she lived a mild-mannered existence teaching high school chemistry and biology.

During the first few years of teaching, everything seemed to be going fine. Around year seven, however, Steph noticed her first inkling that her job wasn't a lifetime fit. "I got an icky feeling deep down in my gut that this wasn't what I was supposed to be doing with my life. Within a couple years, I felt hopelessly trapped by the four walls of my classroom."

During this internally tumultuous time, an unexpected wakeup call came during an online athletic mastermind course. Steph entered the class prepared to discuss the difficulties of competition and the challenges of being an athlete. "I was really surprised," she recalls, "when the mastermind group started off by asking us to rank our satisfaction in aspects of life outside of the gym.

"When I had to rank my work and career, it was at once eye-opening and scary. I knew I had been feeling uneasy at work, but it was still mostly in the back of my mind. The exercise of thinking about career satisfaction really crystallized for me what I had known for a while.

"I finally owned up to the fact that I was not happy at my job and that something needed to change."

By the end of that year, her "hobby" blog where she had been posting recipes for two years started to gain some traction.

"Friends were asking me for nutrition advice, and I was spending the weekends posting recipes. So, I hatched a plan. I would combine my formal education in science, years of teaching experience, and love of food into a new career."

A solid intention, but with one major problem: "I had no freaking clue how it was actually going to happen.

"I realized I didn't have the time to keep teaching and to really take my business to the places I dreamed it could go. I also knew the changes that needed to happen wouldn't happen overnight."

Over the next few years, Steph committed to realizing her dream. She became a nutritionist, saved money to improve her website, and enrolled in a two-month online business and marketing program.

By the end of spring in 2013, she took a big step toward her goal when she sent a letter of request for an unpaid leave of absence during the upcoming school year.

"I decided to work with a life coach because I had another major life change in the works: I was going to move to Scotland for four months to live with my fiancé and work on Stupid Easy Paleo. The thought of moving and changing careers was daunting. I was faced with a lot of excitement, but I was also apprehensive. My coach helped me work through some of my doubts and get clearer about what I really wanted in life.

"After a year away from the classroom, I officially resigned. That was in June 2014. It took me more than three years to finally quit, but I'm incredibly happy I did."

Even with a solid plan and dedication to taking the necessary steps, Steph still had a major obstacle she needed to overcome: her own fears.

"I had every thought going through my head—What will happen if I quit my job and my business fails? Is it smart to leave a stable career? What will people think of me? How am I going to make it all work?

"My 'what if' mentality was keeping me from taking action on certain things, like writing my letter to ask for a leave of absence. Basically, I got stuck.

"I became extremely indecisive and even though I knew what I wanted in my heart, my brain tried to talk me out of it for practical reasons. Simply put, I was trying to play it safe."

Her coaches helped her understand that even small steps represent progress. "They reminded me that I didn't have to figure it out all at once. I did a lot of journaling, reflecting, and planning. I was able to take action on what I wanted and accepted that it was okay to make decisions even if I was afraid.

"I learned that worrying about things that haven't happened is a poor use of my time and energy. As a self-employed person, I really need my time and energy. They are my most precious resources.

"Now I try to focus on making the best decisions I can with the information at hand instead of basing them on some imaginary scenario I play out in my head. That doesn't mean I'm perfect, but making mistakes doesn't make me weak or stupid. I've come to accept that I'll always be learning, and what matters most is how I choose to deal with mistakes."

Her willingness to keep pushing forward has paid off. The Stupid Easy Paleo brand has spread beyond the blog itself. With an award-winning cookbook, coveted workout apparel, and continuing media attention for her work, Steph has created a name for herself in the fitness world.

"The outcome is that I now work for myself doing the things I want to. I'm following my passion."

In sharing the top three lessons from her own experience, Steph says confidently, "First, take action toward your goal, even when the steps are tiny. Baby steps are still progress. Second, surround yourself with supportive people, and get to know others in your niche. Finally, stay true to who you are. You'll be tempted to do what everyone else is doing, but you have to figure out what works for you and do it on your own terms."

Steph's integrity and big heart shine through everything she does. Her secret to success? "Help people by solving problems for them, consistently offer amazing content, and be a damn nice person." And you know what? It's worked.

"I love that I'm doing something to positively impact the world around me. Most importantly, I feel like I'm living the version of my life that I always dreamed of."

"Believe in others and
they will believe in you."

LINDSAY HADLEY

Stevie Wonder, Jay Z, No Doubt, The Roots, Alicia Keys, John Mayer, Foo Fighters, Kings of Leon, John Legend, Band of Horses—the list of past entertainers goes on. In late September every year, thousands stream into New York's Central Park to listen to some of the world's greatest artists. Concertgoers do not purchase tickets for the event, however. They earn entrance by joining a movement to end extreme poverty.

Since 2012, the annual Global Citizen Festival is the culminating event for thousands who have spent months volunteering, signing petitions, educating themselves, and spreading awareness. The event is timed to coincide with the United Nations General Assembly as a public call to action. In the words of its organizers, "The Global Citizen Festival is much more than a flashy concert where people talk about global issues. Rather, it's a flashpoint in a broader campaign for systemic policy change."

The concert has had enormous reach since its first year when it became the largest charity syndication to date with three billion media impressions worldwide. Viewers can watch their favorite musicians perform and simultaneously witness world leaders commit enormous resources to address poverty. Just as importantly, the novel approach of awarding tickets for action fosters mainstream awareness of the pressing issue. With more than 800 million views across social media in the first year alone, the innovative tactic is working.

"You can have everything in life you want if you will just help other people get what they want," said the motivational speaker Zig Ziglar. Lindsay Hadley realizes the power of this mantra and possesses a special talent for motivating engagement in a world where countless causes vie for support. She was one of the executive producers of the Global Citizen Festival in its first two years—a core player in a small but powerful team who brought the concept to life.

Lightning in a bottle would be an apt description of Lindsay. She exudes warmth and a spark for living that lights up her corner of the world. She chooses her goals carefully and once committed, she is unstoppable. Her relentless energy and drive are guided by a fiery dedication to improve the world around her.

Given Global Citizen's unprecedented success, it is hard to believe that only two years prior, Lindsay was questioning her ability to produce events at all.

In 2010, she organized an all-day acoustic festival in her hometown to raise funds for an organization working to combat human trafficking. She dedicated countless hours to planning and logistics while also balancing her role as the mother of two children—a toddler and a newborn.

"Despite giving it my all, the event was not a financial success," she recounts. "I'll never forget returning home after the concert at 4 a.m. and falling prostrate on the floor. I was exhausted and overwhelmed. I cried bitter tears of disappointment. I felt I had failed as a leader. I thought, 'Why did I think I was capable of such an ambitious undertaking?'

"Then, in my despair, I suddenly felt the words, 'This is not about you. This is about the children you were trying to help.' I picked myself up off the floor and decided to do what I could to make things right.

"We organized another event a few months later in an attempt to recover from the financial loss. With a new perspective, I was able to see all the good that had come from our previous work. I had fostered some important connections during that time, including one with a friend of Sumner Redstone, the chairman of Viacom. At the second event, Redstone donated $1 million to our cause. For me, that check was more than an unbelievable donation. It symbolized the way our failures can contribute to our ultimate successes if we allow them to."

Not only did Lindsay organize a second event to turn her failure around, she also used the moment as a learning opportunity.

"Fresh off of the disappointment of my first music festival, I cold-called one of my heroes," she says. "I sought advice from Bill Fold, co-founder and creator of the Coachella music festival.

"Looking back, I'm surprised by my audacity to ask such a busy and important person for a few moments of his precious time, but he gave it to me. He shared invaluable advice and wisdom. He even invited me to California to see his proven tactics firsthand. I took him up on the offer and he opened his Rolodex to me, introducing me to some of my most important contacts. I had nothing to offer him, yet he went out of his way to help me be successful. We've been dear friends ever since."

Years later, Lindsay asked Bill to partner on the Global Citizen Festival. "I'm sure he never imagined that the young woman he helped years before would become a colleague and go on to produce such a huge and successful event, but that isn't why he helped me. He did it because he could. If he hadn't, I wouldn't be where I am today."

Between the year of learning in 2010 and the enormous success of 2012, Lindsay embarked on a project that at first glance seemed impossible.

"I was living in Australia at the time and the Global Poverty Project solicited me to help produce a concert. They wanted to put polio eradication on the agenda of an upcoming meeting of Commonwealth leaders. If they could show that polio eradication had a strong constituency, the Australian Prime Minister would raise the issue at the meeting.

"Michael Sheldrick, a 23-year-old law student at the time, told me of their idea to petition signatures in exchange for concert tickets. I asked how big of a budget they had for the concert. He sheepishly shared that they had none. I asked about the size of their team. He made an effort to dance around the fact that there were only four people able to work on the event.

"My first inclination was that this would be too heavy of a lift. We only had four months to make this happen. I was terrified, but my gut told me I should jump in.

"So, with a tiny but remarkably effective team, I produced 'The End of Polio Concert' in Perth. We held it on the eve of the leaders' meeting. With support from Bill Gates, Hugh Jackman,

Donna Karan, former Prime Minister Kevin Rudd, and John Legend, we got extensive media coverage. 30,000 people signed the petition.

"At a press conference the next morning, the Australian Prime Minister announced a contribution of $50 million for polio eradication, which was matched by other government leaders and the Gates Foundation for a total of $118 million."

This momentous achievement demonstrates Lindsay's "get-back-up-on-the-horse" mentality. If she had dwelled in the space of self-doubt following her first concert or wasted that opportunity to seek out advice, it is very likely she would not have succeeded in Perth, or even had the courage to take on such a task in the first place.

That isn't to say she is impervious to obstacles. In fact, she admits to a challenge familiar to many. "I care far too much about what people think of me," she confides. "One of my better qualities is that I care immensely about other people and as a result, their opinions matter a great deal to me. At times, I suffer from anxiety about failing or letting people down, which can inhibit a clear mind about the best way forward.

"While I cannot say I have overcome this challenge entirely, I know that when I focus on the value of those around me, I become far less concerned with what they might be thinking about me."

This approach of valuing others is at the heart of three priceless lessons Lindsay has learned over the years.

"First, believe in others and they will believe in you. The best part of this ideology is that you don't have to believe in yourself to start, at least not right away. I've found that believing in others is easier to do and it keeps the focus off my doubts and fears. Then, as others begin to believe in you, you will start to believe in yourself.

"Second, never view other people as vehicles to reach your goals. Whether you're dealing with donors, volunteers, employees, family members or friends, you're dealing with people, and people are not disposable. Good relationships should always be your priority. None of your accomplishments could ever make up for damage done to a relationship. Everyone you meet should know how valuable they are.

"Third, anchor your heart at home. No matter where life takes you, you will never regret making your loved ones the cornerstone of your life. Professional opportunities will come and go, but your relationships with loved ones are a once-in-a-lifetime opportunity."

Lindsay continues to find ways to bring people and relationships to the forefront. Her newest initiative, Time Machine, seeks to unite people, causes, and brands through meaningful experiences beyond the screen. As with her previous successes, the mobile app will engage users, reward positive actions, and raise awareness of worthy causes. In short, the unique approach will help everyone involved get what they want and continue to fill Lindsay's life with the elements she loves most. "I thank heaven every day for modern technology, which affords me the opportunity to work from home, because no matter what worthy project I am involved in, none of it matters in comparison to my greatest life project—being the mother of two energetic little boys."

"Allow time for everything to fall into place and keep your passion in the meantime."

SAM SAVERANCE

You would need more than 20 years to eat at all of New York City's restaurants. That's eating out for three meals a day, seven days a week. With so many thousands of restaurants in the city, it is a serious feat to be named as one of Zagat's seven "best things we ate in NYC in 2014." Bunna Cafe's combo plate made the list—not bad for a restaurant that opened in February of the same year.

The concept of Bunna Cafe was born three years prior at a summer rooftop party in Brooklyn. Eager to share the hospitality and warmth he had recently experienced in Ethiopia, Sam Saverance gathered 200 people to break injera bread together, perform a traditional coffee ceremony, and dine on the rich vegan dishes characteristic of the East African nation.

Sam didn't start out with an aim to be in the restaurant business. He started out in finance and then worked as a graphic designer for 10 years. It was through this lens that he first experienced Ethiopia. He traveled to the country to start a small business incubator for graphic design. As a lone traveler, he felt welcomed into the country with open arms.

Although his business venture didn't move forward, the spirit of generosity he felt made a real impact on him.

"I would go into restaurants and easily strike up conversation with the first person I met," he recalls. "Soon, I was being invited for dinner at people's homes. There is such a rich culture of hospitality and they take great pride in that tradition. I wanted to bring that authentic spirit of openness back home with me."

Upon returning to the United States, Sam was committed to sharing the side of Ethiopia that so charmed him. He wanted to provide a genuine experience of the country and alter preconceived notions of the region.

There was only one small catch. He didn't know how he wanted to do it.

He started by building a makeshift hut to host a traditional coffee ceremony for friends. He invited over a hundred people to share the drink—called bunna—and sample classic Ethiopian dishes. It was there on the rooftop, amidst a spirit of connection and celebration, that the idea for Bunna Cafe was born.

Apart from three days working at a Chinese restaurant, Sam had no prior experience in the food industry. His vision for an Ethiopian restaurant was guided only by a desire to share the unique qualities of a country he had grown to love. Early on, he teamed up with two Ethiopians living in New York—the driven and efficient Liyuw who brought years of management expertise to the venture, and the warm and generous Kedega who brought her delicious recipes honed through years of cooking for a large family.

Together, Sam and his partners started out slowly with weekend pop-up restaurants on backyard bar patios and dinner parties in private apartments. Bite by bite, they grew a fan base drawn to the rich, flavorful dishes and welcoming atmosphere.

Eventually, their product was in such high demand that Sam and his team often juggled multiple events in a day. On one of these days, he learned an invaluable lesson about what it means to grow a business.

The team had lined up three events in succession—two pop-ups in Brooklyn with a coffee ceremony in Manhattan sandwiched in between. The coffee ceremony was an especially important moment because one of the city's most renowned chefs would be attending.

As luck would have it, the first event in Brooklyn ran late. As the team crawled through Manhattan's notorious traffic, Sam remembers the anxiety of the moment. "We were so tense and silent you could practically hear the blood flowing through our veins. It was absolutely the worst feeling."

Eventually they arrived at the event space, only to be greeted by the chef's livid manager and malfunctioning equipment. "It was a disaster and we felt terrible," Sam laments. "I'm sure the public thought everything was fine, but for us it was a catastrophe. We were so discouraged. We felt like forgetting the whole idea."

Rather than throw in the towel, the team drove to their next event and discussed the experience en route. They agreed it was a valuable lesson in not biting off more than they could chew. The evening pop-up was a great success and they moved on from the afternoon's disappointment, learning from the experience but not allowing it to alter their course.

"It was a good lesson in not letting one incident dictate how you feel about everything you're doing," Sam says.

By late 2013, Bunna had garnered enough of a following to establish a permanent setup. They started by opening a lunch counter in a cozy soul-food restaurant in Brooklyn. For reasons unrelated to Bunna, the soul-food restaurant went out of business a few months later. It was an opportune moment for the team to take over the lease.

Sam recalls the trepidation he felt about making such an enormous financial commitment. "The place needed a lot of work and the location was not ideal. It was a risky move given our limited funds at the time."

However, there was a deeper intuition signaling that this was the perfect chance to grow. "It felt like the opportunity was being handed to us on a platter. It was the optimal situation if we were ever going to open a brick-and-mortar restaurant.

"Throughout this experience, I've learned that you don't force an opportunity," says Sam. "You create the momentum—like we did with our first rooftop party and hundreds of subsequent events—but then you sit back, do what you do, and wait for the right opportunity to come. When it arrives, that is when you pounce.

"You must combine patience with persistence. I'm often fearful that if I don't move 100 miles an hour to finish something, I'll lose interest. I fear that if I don't push something hard, the drive will go away. The reality is that you have to allow time for everything to fall into place and keep your passion in the meantime."

Throughout the winter months, Sam and his team worked nonstop to prepare the space for February's opening. In between running their last few pop-ups and overseeing renovations, they also launched an Indiegogo campaign to raise funds for a few key improvements.

In the final hours before opening, it was all hands on deck. Friends who had been with Bunna since the beginning were busy with finishing touches indoors while Sam, his brothers, Liyuw, and other friends struggled to hang a 300-pound canopy outside during the middle of New York's infamous polar vortex.

Sam laughs as he recounts the story. "Here we were holding this massive structure 12 feet up in the air and we simply couldn't get the nails in. We were freezing, practically getting frostbite, and having no success. Finally, we decided to leave the project for another time. I'm sure we looked ridiculous as we maneuvered the massive awning through the restaurant into the backyard. My brothers have been so supportive throughout this venture, but there are moments like this when things can get comically heated between us."

The anecdote is a small snapshot illustrating another lesson Sam lives by. "Always have partners," he advises. "Always, always, always—unless you're doing something no one can complement or if the project is very small. Otherwise, you need someone there to bounce ideas off of and to tell you when you're doing something wrong."

By the time they opened their doors, the team had invested everything into making the restaurant operational. Savings from previous events and all funds from the Indiegogo campaign were spent readying the space for business.

Given this upfront investment, Sam recalls the first few months as feeling "tenuous."

"Our biggest challenge was keeping the doors open in the beginning," he admits. "With the substantial early costs, we really didn't know if we were going to make it. We were also still waiting on our liquor license, which we knew was a drawback for diners."

Although they originally had misgivings about the restaurant's location, the neighborhood was precisely what saved them during this period. "We are surrounded by yoga studios," Sam explains. "Given that we have such healthy dining options, as well as delicious juices and teas, it is the perfect fit for the clientele. We had a great crowd in those early days, and nobody cared that there was no booze!"

Their devoted following also played an important role. "People learned we were open in a permanent location and sought us out. We've built up a large following over the years and our mailing list was key to our initial success."

Even though the first few months were harrowing, Sam says he wouldn't have done it any other way. That is the final lesson he offers from the experience.

"Don't give away too much of what you have just for the sake of making the next step happen," he recommends. "Don't sell your life away to make your goal a reality. We could have sought investors or taken out loans, but we didn't and it is all ours now. We have full say and that is a powerful position to be in."

Indeed, having full say is what Sam appreciates most about his life. "I love that my life is so wholly mine. I'm not beholden to anyone.

"I love what I do every day. I'm not living to make money and then living life afterwards. My work is my life and I think that is how you know you are truly living. Everything I do is relevant. I can put my whole personality into this and make it something productive."

By nourishing his own soul, Sam is able to provide a fulfilling experience for everyone who visits Bunna. As a throwback to the earliest days, a traditional coffee ceremony is held several times each week under a small hut inside the restaurant. When bunna isn't being prepared there, local bands take the spotlight. The cafe has become not only one of New York's best new restaurants, but also a space that celebrates generosity, playfulness, and camaraderie—three attributes shared by its founder, the lone traveler who began an incredible journey years ago and has finally arrived.

"Pursue and persist.
Just keep getting up."

DAVID WINTZER

"My guess is that 80 percent of people would have quit by now," says David Wintzer of his venture, the first and only banana-flour company in the United States. After hearing his story, one might put the estimate closer to 99 percent.

The long road to success hasn't been for lack of vision or genuine intentions. Indeed, WEDO Gluten Free is committed first and foremost to the health of its customers and making a difference in the world by giving back. Rather, the arduous journey was inevitable because the founders are pioneers in the food industry, forging a new path every step of the way.

In 2008, David traveled to Kenya as part of a humanitarian mission to provide microloans for entrepreneurs. While there, he worked with a group of women—WEDO, or Women Entrepreneurs Development Organization—who produced banana flour using a simple and streamlined process. Green bananas were peeled, sliced, dried, and milled into a smooth, fine flour. No additives, no preservatives—just a wholesome and versatile product for everyday cooking.

After returning home, David explored the market viability of bringing banana flour to the United States. The demand for gluten-free products and Paleo alternatives was on the rise, and banana flour was the perfect replacement for its wheat-based counterpart.

Impressed as he was by the product's unique attributes, David was also motivated by his interactions abroad. "There was such a sincerity and kindness in the way our hosts welcomed us," he recalls. "There was a beautiful exchange of mutual admiration and gratitude that sparked a change in me. It made me want to pursue a path of connectedness and it helped me truly see the world as a whole."

With this perspective, David was driven to promote well-being at home and provide economic opportunities abroad. He teamed up with his long-time friend Todd Francis to create WEDO Gluten Free. Having integrated banana flour into their own diets with positive results, the pair was guided by a belief in the product and their own ability to start a business while doing good in the world.

Introducing a new food product in the United States is no small endeavor. If studying FDA regulations and import specifications seems yawn inducing, imagine combing through these details for two years. David invested countless hours in self-education on the subject, all while sustaining full-time work to save enough funds to launch the venture.

Even with his newfound expertise, the next few years were complicated by setbacks.

Hoping to source from the women he had worked with in Kenya, David invested a summer abroad and thousands from his savings to build a small production factory in the country.

He spent long days overseeing construction, guiding contractors on strict specifications to bring the building up to code. Away from the construction site, he spent time securing operating documents, whiling away afternoons waiting for approvals. When specialized equipment arrived in the capital, he made long trips to ensure its safe transport back to the factory, assembling teams of day workers to unload the unwieldy machinery.

After months of investment, everyone had high expectations for the new facility. The output needed to be sufficient to fill large containers that would make shipping costs viable. The flour also needed to be produced quickly enough to hold a long shelf life after distribution. After several weeks of touch-and-go operations, they discovered the output was not adequate on either front.

Short of establishing a second facility, there was no option but to shutter the operation and look elsewhere. "Breaking this news to our suppliers was one of the most difficult and heart-wrenching conversations I've ever had," says David, "let alone the immense blow to WEDO's progress."

He began the search for an alternative and found a supplier in the Philippines. At this point, all of the founders' savings had been spent, so they looked to family and friends for loans and invested everything into a large order from a company there.

While waiting for the delivery, David and his team devoted their time to securing product orders. They contacted grocery stores and food suppliers, restaurants, and bakeries. Dozens of new customers were eager to test the flour.

On the day of the expected shipment's arrival, David got a call from the port authorities. There had been a leak in the shipping container and mold had spread throughout the cargo. No bag was salvageable. The entire consignment was useless. The authorities wouldn't even allow the shipment to be unloaded.

"It was absolutely crushing," David recalls. "We had dedicated years to making this a reality and we had to admit defeat in that moment. All of our customers were expecting the product and we failed them. We had overpromised and under delivered."

To say they were back at square one would be generous. After nearly five years of effort, the team had no product, they owed money, and they still needed reliable suppliers.

They were able to secure a small investment to travel to India, Ecuador, Peru, and back to the Philippines to meet with several producers. Eventually, they found suppliers in South America who were equipped to meet their needs. At last, WEDO was ready to place its third order.

The only trouble was that every last penny of the investment had been spent on visiting the facilities.

At this point the team turned to Kickstarter. After exhausting all other avenues, they hoped crowdsourcing would provide the necessary jumpstart to get WEDO off the ground.

While this period may have been a low point, one wouldn't know it by watching their Kickstarter video. At once comical and informative, the short film follows David through his parents' garage as he "slices" bananas with a power saw and "dehydrates" them with a blow dryer before "milling" them with an antiquated device. It seems his deadpan expression will break into a smile at any moment, revealing the lightness and humor he seeks to infuse into WEDO's marketing.

Being able to take this quirky, playful approach is one of the elements David enjoys most about running his own company. "I love the freedom to express myself. I don't have to ask for permission or wait for someone to tell me the approach is right or wrong. That's how I know I'm successful in spite of any outward measure of success—I'm able to explore my own creativity and bring it fully to life."

Thanks to this genuine approach, WEDO had an enormously successful campaign. Seven hundred backers supported them with $35,000—enough to secure another shipment and enter the next phase of growth.

Looking back, David believes the company's current success is due in large part to all of the bumps along the way. "We are living proof that it isn't easy, but also that good things come to those who wait. You have to pursue and persist. You have to keep getting back up."

In fact, the idea of not getting back up has always been more frightening to David than failure. "There would have been so much more pain if I hadn't tried," he says. "There would have always been the terrible question, 'What if?'"

David doesn't allow himself to ask that question very often. Even though it may be intimidating, he never lets fear stop him from reaching out for help when necessary. "One of the biggest lessons I've learned is how often people say yes," he says.

"Recently we reached out requesting advice from a prominent expert by sending a handwritten card with a package of banana-flour cookies. She is at the top of her field and especially busy, but she gave us almost an hour of her time and opened a lot of doors for us. The package we sent was simple, but the gesture was genuine. If you have a sincere story and great product, people believe in you."

Now in over 400 stores, WEDO banana flour is finally having the impact David always envisioned. "We often hear from customers telling us how important the product has become in their diet—not just as a substitute, but as a staple in improving their health. These stories thrill me. Knowing we are making a difference makes my heart sing."

It isn't just the customers who benefit. For every product sold, WEDO donates a portion of the profits to the World Food Program. This decision was made early on, before banana flour was even on the shelves. Since day one, the company's founders have been committed to giving back.

The other element present since WEDO's earliest days is David's tenacious drive for self-improvement. He consistently invests in himself. Every month he sets aside three percent of his income to spend on business-related education like magazines and books. He is committed to expanding his knowledge both within his field and as an entrepreneur.

"You can't become content in success," David cautions. "I believe in the idea that success is never owned. It is rented. Rent is due every single day. If you become successful and then complacent, the game is over."

This voracity for constant improvement will ensure that WEDO continues to grow. Now that it has proven itself as a pioneer in the food industry, the company can explore new frontiers for distribution and expansion. "Success will follow if you follow your heart," David believes. Indeed, that strategy has helped him stay the course when so many others would have given up long ago.

"You have to believe in yourself if you
want to make your dreams come true."

STEPHANIE HOCK

Bright, colorful, and optimistic—these three words perfectly describe Stephanie Hock and her paintings. She loves capturing the fleeting moments of life and finding beauty in unlikely places, so it's hard to picture that Stephanie's path to living her dream was once blocked by her own imagined limitations and the darkness of self-doubt.

Stephanie now has a successful career as an acrylic impressionist painter. Looking back at her home and school life while growing up, it's not surprising that she ended up in such a creative field.

"My mom is an artist and my dad was always expressing himself through writing and music," she recalls. "Creativity was definitely encouraged in our home."

In 10th grade, Stephanie took an aptitude test. Her high scores in the arts—contrasted by average scores in every other subject—sealed the deal. By the time she entered university, she declared herself an art major. "I always figured I'd pursue art in college, long before I set foot on campus," she says.

College proved to be a challenging time despite the opportunities to explore a wide variety of disciplines within the larger scope of her major.

"I went into college with a firm plan. I was going to study graphic design, because I thought that was the only way I could make money as an artist. But my heart wasn't in it. I loved some aspects of it, but deep down I wanted to create something with my hands. I felt disconnected from the computer screen in front of me."

Thinking back to those years, Stephanie recalls the mental crisis she faced. "There's a myth in the world that artists can't make money. Everyone throws around the term 'starving artist' like it's some sort of universal truth. During those years in college, I kept thinking, 'What am I doing here? How am I going to make a living?' I let my fears get to me."

The battle in her mind led Stephanie to explore other degree options. "I considered changing majors entirely. I had other interests, but when I thought of doing something else, I just felt sad. My heart wasn't in it.

"Being an artist was part of my identity. When I took that away, I lost some of me."

Despite the feelings of doubt, Stephanie stuck with the art degree. She figured her college experience would probably culminate in a job unrelated to her field. "Art could be my hobby," she conceded. "I would find another way to earn a living."

Perceived restrictions for making a career as an artist were only half the battle. Despite her obvious talent, there was another glaring frustration that took its toll on Stephanie's fortitude.

"Art is really subjective. That becomes a problem when you're in a setting where professors give out grades. You are constantly being compared to your peers. My teachers didn't give out a lot of A's. They gave a lot of B's and C's. I felt really frustrated that I couldn't achieve the same grades as my peers. Being constantly compared to others stunted my self-esteem and shot down my confidence."

By her senior year, Stephanie felt burned out. She had taken nearly every kind of art class offered, but it wasn't until her last semester that she finally took a painting class.

"At that moment, I felt like I found my place. Finally! This was the medium I was excited to create in. I loved it. The problem was that I was at the end of my college career and I was ready to just be done. Maybe if I had discovered painting early on, things would have been different—but I didn't have the time to really develop the skill.

"When I graduated, I remember looking at my classmates. I figured they would be great artists and I would go off and do something else," she says.

That's exactly what she did.

Stephanie put away her paints and brushes for several years. She got an office job that was safe and comfortable. "I earned my living, but I didn't feel passionate about what I was doing. It was actually a really dark period. I felt like I missed my calling in life."

Over the next few years, Stephanie's fear of not being good enough, along with her frustration at not being able to create the work she envisioned, kept her from pursuing artwork seriously.

Then one day, she was given a small gift that fed her artistic soul.

"My husband's wedding present to me was three tubes of high quality paint. He loved that I was an artist and pushed me to pursue my dreams. He believed in me more than I believed in myself and that made all the difference. I held on to that tiny ray of belief and thought, 'Maybe I can do this.'"

The seed of hope grew as Stephanie began to re-explore her passion for painting. "For years I just painted for myself. I wasn't confident in what I was doing, but I was trying. I was putting in the hours."

Six years into her marriage, Stephanie was invited to participate in a local art show. With nothing to lose, she agreed to contribute a piece to the event. "The show was produced by a friend who I wanted to support. I finished the painting just in time, but I wasn't pleased with it at all. It was yet another frustrating project because the finished piece didn't look anything like I had hoped."

Despite the frustrations, the art show proved to be a defining moment.

"At the show I talked to a friend who had presented a beautiful piece of work. Everyone was going crazy over it and I asked her for advice. I wanted to know how I could get better.

"She told me to reach out to professionals I admired to see if they offered workshops or opportunities to shadow them in their studio. She also recommended a book, *The Artist's Way* by Julia Cameron, that has helped other blocked artists break free."

Stephanie followed through. The friend's recommendations were spot on. When she reached out to her favorite artist, Carole Wade, she learned Carole would be offering a workshop in the following weeks.

Stephanie leapt at the opportunity. "I learned so much. I was so inspired. At one point during the workshop, Carole complimented my work. That was huge. This amazing painter who I admired was saying good things about my work. It gave me hope.

"All those doubts from college started to fall away. My fears were being replaced with dreams. 'Maybe I can do this,' I thought. 'Maybe I am good at this.'"

After the workshop, everything began falling into place.

"It's crazy when the thing you *want* to do lines up with what you feel like you *should* do. I was excited that maybe I really could pursue my passions. I watched in wonder as doors opened for me. For example, slots became available in workshops with artists who were perfect for my style and artistic goals."

Still, Stephanie had plenty of reasons to hold off on her dreams. She was pregnant with her fourth child, living with her family in her parents' basement, and juggling the demands of three active children all under the age of four. Still, she had a feeling deep in her gut that she needed to act at that moment.

"The funny thing about being a professional artist is that there is no moment when someone decides you are a professional. Ultimately, you have to change your own mindset and treat yourself as one."

Recognizing the power of personal beliefs, Stephanie chose to increase the faith she had in her own abilities. "I stopped buying student-grade paints and brushes and began buying the professional grade instead. It sounds silly, but that change was huge. I created a website. I got a business license. I made business cards. I entered paintings into juried shows alongside other professional artists. And as soon as I started seeing myself as a professional, my work actually got better. It wasn't perfect, but I was consistently proud of my art for the first time."

It would have been easy to let excuses keep her from making the leap. With vigorous demands at home, it seemed illogical to add "working artist" to the list of the many roles she was balancing.

"I remember thinking, 'How can I possibly pursue this path at this point in my life? I must be crazy.' But I felt like I could either wait until my children were grown to pursue the thing I love, or I could pursue it alongside the chaos. If you wait for everything to line up perfectly, you'll never take the leap. I've learned that great things can happen even in inconvenient seasons.

"It's taken a lot of sacrifice, team work, and balance, but now I am merging the two careers I've always dreamed of: being an artist and a mother."

Once she believed this course was possible, Stephanie had to make it real by putting in the effort.

"The thing about pursuing your dream is that there are days when it doesn't feel like a dream. It just feels like a lot of work," she says with a laugh. "You won't always be compensated at the beginning, but if you believe in yourself and put in the time, you can earn a living doing what you love, even as an artist."

When asked if she would do anything differently, she recognizes the dark period following college. "I wish I hadn't lost those years," she admits. "I wish I would have had the confidence to keep pushing with the things I love and not let other people's opinions influence what I thought I could do with my life.

"You have to have confidence in your own work. Don't hide behind insecurities or excuses. Success is slow. Be professional and be yourself. Stand firm on your feet and show the world that you are good at what you do. Convince them you are worth it, because you are."

"Don't get scared by the bigness
of your vision. Just take the first step."

LILLY BERELOVICH

In a world constantly bombarded by information, clarity is a rare commodity. It is precisely the precious asset Lilly Berelovich works tirelessly to provide her clients every day.

At Fashion Snoops, the company she founded 15 years ago with her husband, Itay Arad, Lilly guides a team of more than 60 employees worldwide in forecasting global trends. They take in all the world's lovely chaos and make sense of it for those in the marketing and creative industries. By synthesizing cultural influences like fashion, art, and technology, the company provides unique insights on what customers want next.

"We translate the overwhelming amount of data to provide companies with a foundation for innovation," explains Lilly. "We point them in the right direction and save them time by guiding them to follow the right trends."

While Lilly has honed a skill for predicting consumer preferences as far as two years into the future, she never predicted she would be where she is today.

"It was never in my plans to start a business," she says. "I was a trained fashion designer and that was definitely the career I wanted. I worked in the industry in Montreal and New York for many years and loved it."

Though she found her perfect career match early on, it didn't necessarily end in happily ever after. In the late nineties, her husband's job required the couple to relocate to Boston. Lilly describes the move as "horrible." She adored life in New York and though she was able to continue working at her design firm from afar, it was difficult to leave the city behind.

Unbeknownst to her, however, the move would provide the opportunity to invent what she now describes as her "dream job"—Chief Innovation Officer at Fashion Snoops.

"The move forced me to look at what I could create on my own," she says.

She and Itay created a tool that harnessed the emerging Internet to address a pressing need Lilly had identified in her field.

"Great design involves a lot of research to understand the trends," she explains. "In the pre-Internet age, this required extensive travel devoted to information gathering, in addition to time spent designing. As we began to understand the potential power of the Internet, we had a light-bulb moment. It was the perfect tool to deliver valuable content to designers' desks and save them from having to gather it on their own. This was the earliest days of the technology and it was really a breakthrough."

By combining Lilly's design acumen and Itay's business expertise, the couple knew they could provide a powerful resource to designers and other experts looking to stay steps ahead of shifting trends. It was on this premise that Fashion Snoops was born in 2000.

They started the business while holding full-time jobs. In their spare time, they built the small company from scratch. On weekends and evenings, they devoted hours to creating their platform and giving life to a concept that had the potential to transform the industry.

A year after Lilly and Itay launched their business, the startup where Itay worked closed shop. At that point, the couple had a decision to make. He could find another job or commit to their company full-time. They chose the latter option. Confident their idea was a good one, they moved back to their beloved New York to grow the business.

"When the opportunity came, we fully committed ourselves to making it a reality. We jumped in with full force," she says.

Today, Fashion Snoops is a leader in the field, advising tens of thousands of users in more than 40 countries. Leading global brands and retailers look to them for expertise and seek out the company's holistic perspective on emerging trends.

"We built it piece by piece. We hired members of the team one by one. You figure it out day by day," Lilly says as she describes the company's growth over time.

In addition to daily dedication, another important factor has contributed to their success: they always believed it was possible.

"I deeply believe that by naming your vision, you can make it so," says Lilly. "Not everyone trusts their own word so clearly, but if you have full confidence that it can happen, it will.

"Once you say it, you just have to start walking toward the goal. You can't stand in fear thinking, 'Wow, the vision I named is so big!' Don't look at the bigness of it. Just take the first step. It won't happen overnight, but it will be built.

"Anything is possible," she confirms. "Truly, anything you say is possible."

Lilly labels the final element of her success as the "juice of everything."

"Link whatever you do to what you love," she says. "The creation has to come from your heart."

Lilly has always loved the realms of fashion and design, but some people in her past discouraged her from pursuing a career in the industry. Several teachers told her she couldn't do it, saying she didn't have strong drawing skills and that the patterns she created would be impossible to make.

Ultimately, she used these criticisms to her advantage. "I was most empowered by all of the people who told me I couldn't do it," she says.

These days, she is more concerned about what she wants success to look like. She and her husband have built a vibrant office culture where creativity flourishes, but Lilly says they are still mastering the balance between a business that thrives financially while retaining the positive energy they've worked so hard to foster. "Can we become more aggressive on the sales front and still be a place where people love to work?" she questions. "Success can be accomplished in so many ways. We've definitely achieved it in certain areas. The challenge now is to bring it into every aspect of the business."

This is a subject on which she offers advice. "If we could go back and do one thing differently, we would have raised money early on. If we had, we would be playing a different game at this point. There is no need to do it on your own. Bring others along to invest in the vision."

Despite this lesson learned, Lilly's eyes light up whenever she speaks of her work. "I love every minute of it," she beams. "I'm surrounded every day by creative people who love what they do. It is a wonderful collaboration and a beautiful shared experience.

"The process is so day-to-day. You give your all in every moment and suddenly you're through another year when you look back and say, 'Whoa! Look at what we have built! This is awesome!'"

While clarity of vision is a must to make any dream a reality, it is the million connected moments of dedication and effort that ultimately lead to the destination. No matter the end goal, Lilly knows, the most critical moment of all is taking the first step.

"Follow your dreams, and don't settle for less than what you're capable of."

GARRETT HOYT

Nobody understands quite like a farmer that the best things in life aren't easy. You have to nourish the soil, plant the seeds, and provide sunshine, water, and constant care. You have to weed, mulch, and get down on your hands and knees. You have to get dirty.

And, of course, there's the waiting.

There is no harvest without the work, or the waiting.

Garrett's story is not really about what he does for a "living." His education is in exercise science and he currently teaches at Clark College in Vancouver, Washington. He's good at his job, and he enjoys it. The real story, however, is Garrett's drive to work alongside his family to literally grow the life of their dreams.

In 2006, Garrett owned a small personal-training business in Astoria, Oregon. He and his wife had always dreamed of having their own farm to live a more sustainable lifestyle, but his business just wasn't providing the income they needed to progress toward that goal.

"I could have tried to increase the number of clients I was working with," he says, "but that would have meant spending drastically more time to market in another city nearby. It wasn't worth it, so I went back to school."

His family packed up and headed to Utah. He completed all the requisites for a doctorate in exercise science and had only his dissertation left to graduate. Despite the work invested in the program, Garrett wasn't thrilled with how the PhD program was turning out.

Following his gut, he dropped out.

"We moved to Kentucky where I started working for another company. We lived in an apartment for a bit as we looked for a house with some land so we could try our hand at sustainable living. In our price range, we either had to be a long ways out of town or take something smaller than we really wanted."

With patience, they ended up finding a large lot in town. Everything seemed to be heading down the right road. However, even though Garrett loved his job, the pay wasn't sufficient to build any sort of savings. They felt stalled in their progress toward what they really wanted.

"One day, my wife's sister called. She had an 18-month-old baby and had been put on bed rest during her second pregnancy. They were supposed to be moving and they really needed help. My wife and I wanted to fly out for at least a week to help, but there was no way we could afford tickets for our entire family. It was at that point that we realized we were not in a situation that worked for us."

They decided to create that situation.

In December 2010, Garrett and his family took the ultimate risk. They quit their jobs, sold everything that didn't fit in their travel trailer, and moved across the country.

Garrett, his wife, and their four boys lived in the 30-foot RV as they sought the right situation to grow their dreams.

They lived out of their trailer for just over a year. During that time, Garrett applied for jobs and went to several interviews. Each time, the entire family hooked up the trailer to the van and drove out to the interview location. "The plan was that if we got the job, we would have already moved and we could start saving money immediately until we could afford the property that we wanted."

Not many people are willing to give up nearly everything they own to pursue their dreams, especially if it means living as a family of six in a trailer. As Garrett says, "It was so illogical to leave a decent job while the economy was horrible and move across the country to where I didn't have a job. But it just had to be done.

"During that year, there was a lot of temptation to just take any job. But instead of giving in, I remembered the words of my mother: 'Don't settle.'"

"My mother's advice was actually good," Garrett reflects. "Follow your dreams, and don't settle for less than what you're capable of."

Garrett was eventually offered a part-time teaching gig at a community college, but the pay didn't match up with the high living expenses of that area. He turned down the job at first, but the very next day his family was offered an internship at a small organic farm.

Finally, the right opportunities were aligning.

Garrett had his teaching schedule rearranged so he only had to commute twice a week. The rest of the time he could spend working and living on the farm.

"In exchange for our labor, we were provided a place to park our travel trailer. We loved the work. Communal living was a bit of a challenge at times, but also wonderful. We really learned the meaning of community."

As the winter season approached, and the work on the farm lessened, the Hoyt family began their final search for land they could call their own. After their year-long journey, they purchased five acres just outside Battle Ground, Washington, where they started Five Sprouts Farm (named for their now five children). Garrett continues to teach as they pursue a simple, idyllic, sustainable life.

When asked what he appreciates most about his life, Garrett says, "I love being able to create things on our land. I love that we are planting trees and creating a situation that will improve our area for decades, maybe centuries, to come. I love working together with my family to create our dream. I love growing our own food on our own land."

Of course, there will always be challenges.

"The biggest challenge is being pulled into the real world. The real world provides a regular income and stability, but that isn't the dream.

"While I was working part-time, we were growing produce and selling at the local farmers market for supplementary income. It wasn't much, but we enjoyed the involvement in the community. We enjoyed working together as a family and we had extra time when the job wasn't full-time. While not a great income, it had its benefits.

"Now that my job is full-time, the focus of our farm has changed from annual vegetable production to modeling sustainability in the community. We have a focus on establishing edible perennial plants so that in the future we will be able to show how landscaping can be as much a part of agriculture as an annual garden. We are working toward becoming a resource in the community where people can see sustainability modeled on a practical level."

Garrett still looks forward to every opportunity he has to spend time working in the fields. Their family saves as much money as possible to pay off their property so they can build a house and become debt free. "Then we will be able to focus on sustainability and invest in our future by growing the important things in life—our family and the plants that sustain us."

When asked if he would do anything differently, Garrett admits he would have loved to be able to seek out his dreams earlier in life. "But in reality, the right opportunities weren't available. The timing just wasn't right."

Garrett recognizes how important it is to not give up. Whether it's a timing issue or money issue, he continues to rally the battle cry: "Never settle."

"Sometimes you have to give up good opportunities in order to wait for the right opportunity."

"Put your blinders on
and just be true to yourself."

STEPHANIE FISCHIO

Stephanie Fischio's story of applying to hair school evokes both giggles and sympathy. It is hard to imagine the main character is the same person as the gregarious, self-assured storyteller.

"I was so nervous to drop off my application that when I approached the building, I completely missed the big sign—'Use Other Door.' I stood there shaking the handle and cursing under my breath. Everyone inside was staring at me, wondering why I was struggling with the locked doors." Stephanie tosses her head back in laughter at the memory. "When I finally saw the sign, I was mortified. I walked back to my car and almost drove away!"

She didn't drive away, though, and 15 years later she's doing what she dreamed of since kindergarten. "I distinctly remember when I knew I wanted to cut hair. I was five years old and my Aunt Patsy cut my long hair into a bob. I loved it. I loved every aspect of it. I loved the sound of the scissors, the sensation of lightness, and the way I looked. Even now, when I see photographs from that time, I can tell I was so happy and I felt so good."

Stephanie delights in delivering the same experience for clients in her daily work. "I love transforming someone's world. You wear your hair every day and if you love something you wear every day, it can totally alter your perspective. To transform a person's world and make them happy is absolutely the best feeling."

Though she loves her career, it took Stephanie longer than most to enter the field professionally. "Everyone starts really early, around 18 or even 16. In high school I thought about taking a class, but I didn't because of fear. I was scared of the testing and the social side, knowing that I would have one-on-one conversations with clients. I was painfully shy. For years I'd been doing my family's hair and I was the go-to for friends during prom, but the thought of interacting with strangers every day made me so nervous."

Once out of high school, Stephanie opted for administrative work and managed a real estate agent's office for several years. "A lot of what I learned about architecture during that time transferred into my current work—like principles of elevation and how lines complement one another.

"In that job, I gave the office a 'makeover' by revamping the entire filing system. I loved the feeling of turning something average into something great. Over time I recognized that the art of transformation is what I love most and do best. It dawned on me that, as a stylist, I could do that all the time.

"During this time, I was still doing hair any chance I could. My mind was constantly filled with new ideas—it still is. I would dream about new styles and want to try them out. I couldn't deny any longer that I just needed to go for it, even if I was terrified."

At 26, Stephanie started the program. "I still remember the anxiety I felt before my first appointment. During school, you learn the basics in the back before going out on the floor. I was confident in my skills and I felt ready. Then I walked up to see who was on my books and I thought, 'I'm going to have to talk to this person!' I panicked. I had the technical skills, but not the social part. I really had to work on that.

"Ultimately, I just jumped in with both feet. I'm sure I blushed a lot and people thought I was odd, but eventually I got over it."

Anyone who meets Stephanie today will find it difficult to believe shyness was ever an impediment. Bright-eyed and affable, she has a special talent for reading people in the chair and helping them feel at ease. She laughs easily and listens intently, playing the part of both comedian and therapist.

On the technical side, her confidence comes from an early commitment to succeed in the trade.

"When I started school, the teacher welcomed the class by informing us that only 80 percent of us would graduate and only five percent of us would be doing hair after five years. In that moment, I promised myself I would be part of the five percent."

During her training, she could easily replicate hairstyles from only a picture and won contests for the skill. Written tests, however, were a different story. Stephanie jokes that she barely graduated high school because she was so averse to testing. Always an artist, she preferred creating to rote learning. "Ultimately I passed the licensing exam because I spent hours and hours memorizing all of the rules and regulations. I didn't love that part of it, but you figure out a way to compensate for what doesn't come naturally."

In the end, Stephanie excelled by showing up every day—emotionally, mentally, and physically. "I just wanted to eat, sleep, and breathe it all in," she recalls.

When starting out as a freelance stylist in her first salon, she continued to succeed by always showing up. "Even when I didn't have any appointments, I was there every day in case someone walked in." Over time she built up a steady stream of regulars, many who have stayed with her since the beginning.

The challenges she now faces are not multiple-choice questions or sparsely filled appointment books. In an industry that follows the whims of whatever's trending, Stephanie says her greatest difficulty is witnessing the erosion of unique expression. "It is difficult to see that we are slowly becoming indistinguishable from each other. Naturally we influence each other, and that's a good thing, but I see so many people who give up their personal style to adopt another's. It's been especially striking over the past five years.

"As someone who sees this play out every day, I try to help people embrace what is natural to them. That is when real beauty emanates.

"Put your blinders on and just be true to yourself. You know what that looks like."

Stephanie strives to live by this mantra herself. She still has the stool she sat on all those years ago when Aunt Patsy cut her hair. It is her reminder to follow the passion she discovered early in life, no matter how difficult. It's also a reminder of how far she's come.

"I cheer for late bloomers," she says. "Life doesn't necessarily get easier as you age; you just know yourself better. If you are willing to show up, be true to yourself, and be kind, you'll have success no matter when you enter the game."

"Find what makes you feel alive,
and then do that thing."

PEGGY HACKNEY

They say a picture is worth a thousand words, but what about a gesture? A firm handshake? A nervous tapping of the foot? Movement is all around us, but most of us take for granted this primal language we all share.

As an internationally recognized Certified Laban/Bartenieff Movement Analyst, Peggy Hackney is a master of the science of movement. Like so many of the pioneers of the field, she entered the world of movement through dance. Though she has an impressive resume as a professional dancer, the title itself is too limiting. She is also a scientist, educator, and leader who guides others in discerning and refining the personal, cultural, and even universal language of movement.

There are relatively few opportunities that come to mind for someone has chosen "movement" as their career path. Most don't realize it is even a viable option. Peggy is bringing awareness to an ever-growing field.

Consider just some of the things she's done in this seemingly confined space: she was featured in *The New York Times* for her analysis of candidates' body language during a 2012 presidential debate. She received a grant from the National Science Foundation to research and improve the dynamics of motion capture in animation. She has served on the GreenDot Project team at New York University, a group that is training computers to analyze "movement signatures" of world leaders. She has served in university administrative roles, co-founded an internationally recognized certification program, and worked with individual clients in physical, movement, and massage-therapy settings. She has traveled the world, inspired thousands, and done it all with a skip in her step.

Not bad for a woman who just turned 70.

Each of the versatile endeavors of her career has its own story, but when you step back and view Peggy's entire life, you realize the uniting theme is passion.

"Live and teach from your own 'aliveness.' If you don't, you'll die inside," she says.

In other words, find what makes you feel alive, and then do those things. That, in a nutshell, is what Peggy's story is all about. Her life affirms that there are countless opportunities to create meaningful work from your interests, no matter what they are.

Let's be clear about one thing: it isn't usually easy to pursue the thing you love, especially if it isn't valued by the world.

Peggy speaks briefly about this challenge: "I find it difficult to accept that I am in a cognitive minority." During her schooling, she recognized the tendency for society to focus on the mind and not the body. "The belief at that point was that truth resided in science, and that anyone with intelligence needed to use their brain to discover the answers to life's mysteries."

Peggy has always valued the body's innate intelligence. She started dance lessons at the age of three, and is continuing even now. Still, she struggles with the fact that "most Americans do not value movement as a way of making meaning."

"I went to Duke University to major in chemistry," she says. "But I soon realized that if I majored in chemistry, I would have to spend every afternoon of my college career in the laboratory. The afternoons were when the modern dance classes were taught—so I decided to major in psychology.

"The summer after my freshman year, I attended the American Dance Festival and discovered Rudolf Laban's work, Labanotation, which is a system for analyzing and notating movement. This was a seminal moment for me! Here was a way I could use my analytical mind in relation to my art form."

Laban Movement Analysis (LMA) is a method and language for visualizing, interpreting, and documenting human movement. Upon introduction to the system, Peggy was hooked. Despite LMA's seemingly niche application, she has utilized it to build bridges and relate her passion for movement to a variety of disciplines.

"I have used LMA for 50 years to bring aliveness, vitality, and lifelong creativity to my existence," says Peggy. She speaks about the confidence her work gave her to make connections, both with herself and with people around the world.

"To quote my colleague, Brenton Cheng, I'm dedicated to living a 'high-resolution life,'" she says. She values curiosity, playfulness, and mobility, and never confines her life to any one thing.

When asked what she enjoys most about her life, Peggy says, "I love that I have chosen to make a life that invites me to constantly engage the fullness of my whole self."

Above all, Peggy dances with the changes of life.

"There is not one formula that you can follow to become the perfect person, dancer, teacher, or therapist. Constant change is here to stay," she says. "In other words, nothing is ever set. The moment you attach yourself to a certain result and try to hold onto it, change will happen."

That talent for seeing, creating, and acting on many possibilities has helped Peggy find rich experiences in an undervalued and still developing field. Her career, in many ways, sprung from a desire to do the things she loves, even if that meant creating opportunities that didn't exist before.

"Life is appreciating the changing moment. Life is living in the movement," says Peggy. "Being able to move into action in spite of uncertainty is needed in our fast-paced, constantly changing world."

When asked if she would do anything differently, Peggy says, "I constantly ask myself that question, but so far, the answer has been no. There is no other profession in which I could use my full physicality, my intellect, my feeling self, and my inner spirit.

"Remaining physical in the way I'm used to is becoming more difficult as I age and move away from teaching movement full-time." But Peggy never lets excuses, particularly age, get in the way of pursuing enlivening experiences. Instead of fearing change, she relishes the opportunities to keep moving and commit fully to whatever she is doing. "Since I hate traditional exercise, finding a way to engage my dancing spirit is not always easy. I will continue to teach the Laban work, but my daily artistic work may evolve into painting or some other expression."

Peggy's petite frame is overshadowed by her larger-than-life enthusiasm. Whether teaching, dancing, or discussing the details of rotary function of the hip, her eyes always smile. Radiant and buoyant, she embodies energy. Her continual drive to seek out meaningful experiences has given her a fountain-of-youth power. She breathes life into her work by finding work that breathes life into her.

"We only get one life. We owe it to ourselves to make it the best life possible."

TIM RADJY

Growing up in Switzerland with parents from Bolivia and Iran has given Tim Radjy a unique perspective. From an early age, he's sought to understand the world's inherent interconnectedness in everything from politics to economics.

"When I was 16, a high school friend asked what I wanted to become and I told him I wanted to be a 'generalist.' He laughed and told me that wasn't a career, but even at an early age I understood the importance of big-picture thinking. I wanted to know enough about everything to effectively connect people and ideas. I didn't know exactly what the profession would be, but I knew that's what I wanted to do in life."

Exploring different fields through internships and early studies helped Tim develop an aerial worldview, while leading him closer to a traditional job title. With each experience, he narrowed down the aspects he wanted in his future work.

"I learned key skills during a journalism internship, but I knew the field wasn't the right fit. I wanted to be able to affect the outcome of the story, not just report on it," he says. Two years in law school brought more lessons, but Tim admits, "I went because my parents wanted me to, not through any interest of my own." He switched tracks to study political science, and though he loved the coursework, an internship at the United Nations revealed that the diplomatic route was also not the right path.

Upon graduation, Tim helped his alma mater develop its first career center and after a year of helping others find satisfying work, he finally found his own—in banking.

"I love banking," he says. "It gives such insight into the world and into people. I worked in private banking for seven years and advised some of the world's wealthiest clients. Interacting with them allowed me to see how centuries of entrepreneurship have survived the tides of history."

Though some clients were managing wealth built over generations, Tim and his mentors knew the importance of providing services relevant to the modern day. His bank was one of the first to offer clients an opportunity to become more strategic about their philanthropic interests. By guiding social investors to organizations promoting what they care about, such as environmental protection or human rights, this type of commitment fosters viable solutions to public issues.

With this new service, Tim could synchronize his early interests in world affairs with his expertise in finance. He was finally on his way to becoming a professional generalist.

As he gained more insight into the new sector, he saw immense opportunity in investing in microfinance—loans extended to those often left out of the formal banking system. With these small injections of credit, borrowers can often grow their business or send their children to school. Tim spent long hours working on a proposal for the senior leaders highlighting the potential of this offering. Ultimately, however, his recommendation was not adopted.

"Sometimes being an intrapreneur can be tougher than an entrepreneur," he says. "Innovating inside a large institution can be difficult, especially when you're trying to create an entirely new product line."

Enthused by his opportunities to date, but disenchanted by the rejection of his proposal as well as shifting office politics, Tim felt the time was right to strike out on his own.

Rather than make the move immediately, he stayed at the bank for a year to consider the best next step. "For months I wondered what to do," he recounts. "It took some time for my thoughts to coalesce."

He gained insight in the least likely of places—mandatory military service. As a Swiss citizen, Tim was required to serve in the country's army, but he recognized his skills might best be suited for civil service. Most who take this alternative option work at cultural sites or provide basic community services for the elderly, for example—but Tim took a risk and proposed a different idea directly to the Department of Foreign Affairs' Development Agency. With his Bolivian heritage, fluency in Spanish, and banking background, he explained, he could apply a unique skillset working for the country's development agency abroad.

The agency agreed and Tim spent the next four months assessing and promoting microfinance in Bolivia. While there, he was struck by the financial success of firms providing loans to the country's micro-entrepreneurs. The capital gave them an important stepping stone to opening or expanding small businesses in the country.

By the time he returned to Switzerland, Tim had his business idea. He planned to start a firm specializing in impact investing. Stakeholders would have the opportunity to invest in companies working in areas such as sustainable agriculture, accessible healthcare, and solar technology. For-profit ventures in these sectors address some of the world's most pressing challenges—something that spoke directly to Tim's own heart.

In 2008, Tim established the firm AlphaMundi and set to work recruiting investors and establishing a fund. "Creating the business from scratch was very different than sitting behind a comfortable desk at the bank with support from a legion of financial specialists," he says. "We were in an entirely new field! Impact investing was rare at the time and we had to develop all of the necessary processes and systems to make it viable."

The challenges took nearly a year to figure out. Unfortunately the timing couldn't have been worse. By the time the fund launched in 2009, the world was in the middle of financial meltdown.

"Life is fickle like that," Tim says now with a touch of lightness, though at the time, the reality was far from trivial. "Everything was in place when the crisis hit. Our main investor was forced to pull out, which meant we launched with $3 million instead of $13 million when we opened. We were seriously set back from day one. It took three difficult years to get back on track."

One way Tim and his partners kept the venture afloat was through a temporary philanthropy advising service that guided donors on effective giving. The service quickly grew and was soon generating 10 times the profit of the investment arm of the business.

While the partners and staff were thrilled, Tim knew philanthropic advising was not the service he ultimately wanted to provide. "It was taking so much time that we couldn't develop the investment company we really wanted," he explains. "It was keeping us afloat, but we weren't headed in the right direction."

In the face of intense opposition, Tim worked to convince shareholders that AlphaMundi needed to stop providing the philanthropic services and focus solely on investing. It flew in the face of reason because it meant giving up a reliable income stream to focus on the business unit that was generating barely 10 percent of revenue.

"I could see myself jumping over a cliff with no parachute and no wings, but it was crystal clear that we'd never be able to pursue investing if we were dedicating all of our time to advising donors," Tim says. "We removed all security when we stopped providing the donor services. There were only two possible outcomes in the investing scenario—success or failure."

With the shift in focus, two shareholders withdrew from the company. Tim describes the process of buying them out as "financial gymnastics."

"I looked to everyone for help during this period, because there comes a point when you'll do anything to make it work. Friends and family wanted to support me, but they were wary. They knew their loans couldn't be guaranteed. I had to do things like sell our apartment and draw upon my family's inheritance to refinance the business.

"People urged me to give up. They offered me jobs. It was difficult to keep going, but I was convinced the idea was a good one and I knew failure was not an option."

After two draining years and months of sleepless nights, new investments finally started coming in. By 2013, the fund was slowly rebuilt and AlphaMundi was back to its initial plan of managing $10 million in investment capital.

Now, after six years of intense dedication, the firm has established its credibility in the sector. "We've only lost money on an investment once," Tim says proudly, "and we've made money on 39 deals. Generally, our fund generates a four-percent return for investors." In the still emerging field, these are impressive statistics.

"The best part is that we're investing in transformational companies that are breaking the boundaries and providing services to those who need them most."

For example, one company provides low-income students in Mexico with affordable payment plans for university, enabling a new generation to obtain higher education. Another company has sold more than a million solar lamps in East Africa, providing much-needed light in places where electricity may not be reliable or even available.

These types of examples are the best part of Tim's work. "I love waking up every morning believing in what I do—pioneering self-sustaining solutions to reduce poverty."

As he reflects on the road that finally led him here, Tim offers powerful advice to those ready to embark on their own journeys.

"We only get one life. We owe it to ourselves to make it the best life possible. If you can, take a chance. If you aren't putting others at risk, take a chance and do something you've always wanted to do. Do something that you think is a little impossible, a little crazy. What is the worst that can happen? Even if you fail, at least you'll know you tried.

"There is nothing worse in life than the 'what if' question. If you don't try, you're doing yourself and others a disservice. If you're not living your full potential and you're not happy, it can have a negative ripple effect on those around you.

"When you do take that chance, however, do your homework. There's no substitute for hard work and research. Listen to what other people are doing. Have a test phase. Submit your idea to 100 people who aren't family and friends and ask for honest feedback. Then don't dwell on the negative; just draw lessons from what you hear and move forward."

The final lesson is one that Tim has experienced firsthand and also witnessed through many years in advising clients.

"All of the successful entrepreneurs we worked with at the bank shared one trait—perseverance. Dedication and perseverance always won the day. We often hear 'instant success' stories, but in most cases, success has to be earned. Lucky breaks can't be your business plan."

As one reads Tim's story, it is clear that luck had nothing to do with it. His is a tale of dedication and resilience, innovation and vision. Now, by investing in fellow entrepreneurs the world over, he helps others live their own stories, built on the same themes.

What will your story be?

CONCLUSION

You are more powerful than you think.

Every moment, you are creating something that has the potential to be absolutely amazing—your life. Twenty-four hours at a time, your days are crafted by the things you do, the words you speak, and the thoughts you believe.

History has proven that an individual's actions can shape society, inspire nations, and propel social change. Some may believe power lies in the hands of a select few, but in reality we each have potential to mold our own futures—and that of the world—in meaningful ways. When we unlock that innate strength to live our dreams, we ignite a flame of passion that can spread like a wildfire.

Unfortunately, the idea that we are helpless victims of our jobs can be just as contagious. We have become slaves to the workweek. The unfortunate myth in our society is that work is often joyless. Most people are told to earn their living by casting away ideals and accepting that this is life in the "real world."

From our mass-produced educational system to the "survival of the fittest" work mentality, it can be hard to follow your heart and live life on your own terms. "It's not how things are done," we are told. But what if we could flip that paradigm on its head? What if it *could* be the way things are done?

The ray of hope shines from the fact that there are some people who refuse to follow the norm. As shown throughout the pages of this book, there are people—everyday people—taking a chance on their dreams. They are taking a chance on themselves.

The lessons they share are priceless—lessons of leaving their comfort zone, embracing failure, facing fear, and committing to a vision. At the heart of each story, however, is the most important lesson: each of us has something unique to offer the world.

That includes you. You have something to offer that nobody else can give, talents no one can duplicate. Once we realize this truth, we can redefine work. We can reclaim our lives and stop living for the weekend.

Meaningful work can change the world.

When what we do aligns with what we love, we do more than simply follow our passion. We pave the path for a powerful movement. When we discover who we are at our deepest level and live in honor of that truth, we give permission for others to do the same.

So, the real question is: what is holding you back? What excuses block your path to the life you want to live? What would you do if you couldn't fail? What would you do if you could do anything in the world?

*What kind of person do you want to be?*

The idea of living your dreams may be exhilarating. It may be terrifying. To some, it may seem impossible. For those unsure of their potential, we kindly urge you to open your eyes and see a vision of the life you want to lead. Then take a step. Big or small, it doesn't matter. Just begin walking—run if it feels right. Keep moving forward, even if you are afraid.

Don't let the myriad of excuses keep you from taking that leap of faith. Excuses about lack of money, time, talent, or connections are often fears disguised as reasons not to try. They are hurdles, to be sure, but they can't stop you from progress if you are willing to rise above them. As every person in this book has demonstrated, you can achieve a life you love no matter what. Hard work and perseverance are powerful tools to help you overcome frustration and failure.

Sometimes getting up after failure will be harder than anything you have ever imagined. But the reward for persistence will always be worth it. When you are excited by what you do, the long hours, discomfort, rejection, and setbacks will serve as fuel to ignite your inner strength. Pursuing your vision will leave you with a satisfying feeling that's hard to describe but easy to name.

It's called happiness.

So, the next time the alarm goes off and a new workweek lies before you, what will you do with it? Will you mourn its arrival and hope it passes quickly while you dream of Friday? Or will you embrace it as an opportunity to seize your dreams and claim your right to happiness?

An amazing life is yours for the taking—on Monday and every day of the week.

# LEARN MORE

This book would never have seen the light of day without the time given by those interviewed. We are deeply grateful to them for sharing their stories with us. Learn more about the amazing individuals featured in *Take Back Monday* and how to connect with them at: www.takebackmonday.com/people

# GIVING BACK

We are thrilled to donate half of the proceeds from this book to 20 amazing non-profit organizations chosen by the individuals profiled. To see which organizations were chosen and to learn more about them, visit: www.takebackmonday.com/giving-back

# ABOUT THE AUTHORS

## BECKY BURTON

Becky Burton is a hopeful adventurer. Having lived in Tanzania, France, Ecuador, and New York, she loves every corner of this spinning blue sphere we call home. Her most recent accomplishment is a 160-page love letter to the Big Apple, otherwise known as her first novel. Becky conceives of her stories in real time, meaning she writes and posts a chapter each week based on real events. Through everything she creates, she seeks to celebrate the wonderful privilege of being human. To learn more about Rebecca's novel approach to writing, visit: www.gusmcallibaster.com

## ROBIN KONIE

Robin Konie is best described as "eclectic." Her driving passion in life is following her interests and creating opportunities from them. As a best-selling author, trained dancer, professional blogger, entrepreneur, "retired" university professor, certified movement analyst, mother, and wife, she is not afraid to mix things up and live her dreams fully. With an audience that has reached nearly nine million people through www.thankyourbody.com, five other authored books, and countless teaching opportunities, Robin has helped individuals around the world live healthier, happier, more fulfilled lives. To learn more about Robin, visit: www.robinkonie.com

## Also by Becky Burton (aka Gus McAllibaster)

*The Audacious Magpie*

*The Intrepid Starling*


## Also by Robin Konie

*Improvised: How to create the life you really want.*

*The Clutter Trap: Learn how to organize your life for good!*

*All Natural Living: 75 non-toxic recipes for home & beauty*

*Processed Free: A real food guide to eating healthy*

*Live Pain Free: 60 somatic exercises to enhance mobility*

*and stop chronic pain*

.